Patricia Leary

CHANGING

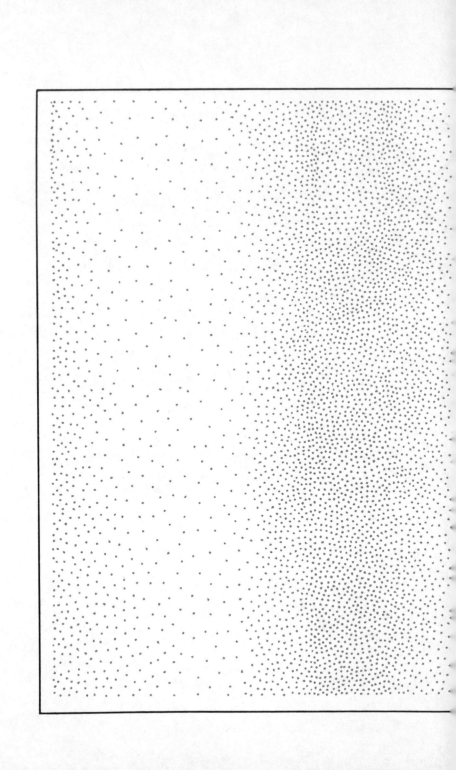

CHANGING

by LIV ULLMANN

ALFRED A. KNOPF NEW YORK 1977

Translated by the author,
in collaboration with
Gerry Bothmer and Erik Friis.

Thank you, David Outerbridge, for caring

THIS IS A BORZOI BOOK
PUBLISHED BY ALFRED A. KNOPF, INC.
Copyright © 1976, 1977 by Liv Ullmann
All rights reserved under International
and Pan-American Copyright Conventions.
Published in the United States
by Alfred A. Knopf, Inc., New York,
and simultaneously in Canada
by Random House of Canada Limited, Toronto.
Distributed by Random House, Inc., New York.
Originally published in Norway as Forandringen
by Helge Ericsen Forlag
Copyright © 1976, by Liv Ullmann.

Library of Congress Cataloging in Publication Data
Ullmann, Liv.   Changing.
Translation of Forandringen.
1. Ullmann, Liv. 2. Actors—Norway—Biography.
I. Title.
PN2768.U4A3213   1977   791.43'028'0924 [B]   76-13167
ISBN 0-394-41148-X
Manufactured in the United States of America

To my daughter, Linn

Sometimes I give names to people in this book,
but most of the time I do not.
Sometimes people will appear with a name
one time and without the next.
But they are all real,
and what I write about them
is what has been part of my life.

CHANGING

I WAS BORN IN A SMALL HOSPITAL IN TOKYO. MAMMA SAYS she remembers two things:

A mouse running across the floor, which she took as a sign of good luck.

A nurse bending down and whispering apologetically: "I'm afraid it's a girl. Would you prefer to inform your husband yourself?"

I AM SITTING HERE, MY THOUGHTS CARRYING ME AROUND the world and within myself, trying to record the voyage on paper.

I want to write about love—about being a human being—about loneliness—about being a woman.

I want to write about an encounter on an island. A man who changed my life.

I want to write about a change that was accidental and a change that was deliberate.

I want to write about moments I regard as gifts, good moments and bad moments.

I don't believe that the knowledge or experience that is part of me is any greater than what others have.

I have attained one dream—and acquired ten new ones in its place. I have seen the reverse side of something that glitters.

It is not the Liv Ullmann people meet in magazines and newspapers that I shall be writing about. Some may think I have left out important facts about my life, but it has never been my intention to write an autobiography.

Ironically, my profession requires daily exhibition of body and face and emotions. Now I feel that I am afraid of revealing myself. Afraid that what I write will leave me vulnerable and no longer able to defend myself.

I am tempted to embroider, to make myself and my surroundings appear nice to win the reader's sympathy. Or to blacken things, to make them more exciting.

It is as if I am not convinced that reality itself is of interest.

"There's a young girl in me who refuses to die," wrote the Danish woman author Tove Ditlevsen.

I live, rejoice, grieve, and I am always struggling to become grown up. Yet every day, because something I do affects her, I hear that young girl within me. She who many years ago was I. Or who I thought was.

It is an eager and almost always protesting voice, although at times faint and full of yearning or sorrow. I don't want to heed it, because I know it has nothing to do with my adult life. But it makes me uncertain.

Some mornings I decide to live *her* life, be something other than what ordinarily is my daily role. I snuggle close to my daughter before she is awake, feel her warm, peaceful breathing, and hope that through her I may become what I wished to be.

Looking back on what I remember of my childhood's dreams, I see that they resemble many I still have, but I no longer live as if they were part of reality.

She who is in me and "refuses to die" is still hoping for something different. No success satisfies her, no happiness hushes her.

All the time I am trying to change myself. For I do know that there is much more than the things I have been near. I would like to be on the way toward this. To find peace, so that I can sit and listen to what is inside me without influence.

NORWAY

My reality this winter consists of many things. Even this: I wake from a doze. My flight is approaching a city. The sun vanishes behind tall mountains. Far below, lights go on in thousands of windows and street advertisements. For a moment I don't remember where I am going. Cities resemble each other as much as the planes that take me to them. It is disquieting that one's destination should be so unimportant. The same women and men will be standing by the same exits and will exclaim the same words of welcome when they see me. People with flowers and kindness, all in a hurry to pack me into a car and drive me to some luxury hotel, where they can abandon me and go home to their own lives. A suite with sitting room and bedroom, deep armchairs upholstered in silk, big windows looking out onto palms and a swimming pool.

Champagne on ice with the compliments of the management. Flowers and baskets of fruit. Hall porters bowing themselves in and out with my luggage and my letters and my telephone messages. Smiles and politeness and the unreality that surrounds it all.

While I smile enthusiastically and thank them.

My reality is also this:

The airplane is circling above a city. There is expectancy in me as I look out into the night. I know it is hot. No need to think of Norwegian homespun and boots for a few days . . . air that calls for no more than a thin blouse.

I shall be awake when everyone at home is asleep.

The stewardesses are busy clearing up after their long trip. They are eager and bustling; we are all infected with the same anticipation.

It has been a long flight. There has been a film and breakfast and lunch and dinner. Trolleys have been trundled in and out with food and fruit, ice-cold drinks, and a woolen blanket to put round me when I want to sleep.

I try to arrange my hair, glad that Hollywood has accepted my "natural look."

At home people will soon be waking up to a dark winter's morning and their feet and bottoms will be freezing, while I am sitting in the shade of a palm, and the feel of the evening air will be sensual, as it never is in Oslo. I shall sleep in a broad, soft bed. Be woken in the morning by a waiter who knows me from earlier visits. He will draw the curtains and let the sun flood into the room, push in a table with breakfast and fresh orange juice. Then he will ask after Linn. Give me a newspaper of a hundred pages and wish me a good day.

It's easy to make me feel secure and happy for a short while. I don't need to be near the man I love. Or Linn. Sometimes the sense of security is within myself.

WHEN I WAS LITTLE I WAS FASCINATED BY THE MOON. Never constant, but faithful, it looked in on me. If I woke during the night, there it hung, pale and mysterious.

When it was quite new and thin, I would stand by the window and curtsy to it three times. Then a wish would come true. If I had been having bad dreams, I would ask the moon that no one I loved would leave me.

Papa had.

I remember sitting alone with him before the operation that was to be his last. Doctors and nurses kept coming and going—there was bustle and preparation around us—yet I felt as if we were alone. When he said goodbye in a strange voice, I knew that we were sharing a secret. I was six and I was trying to be brave and not to cry.

We were living in New York when the two telegrams crossed in the Atlantic. Papa had died of a tumor on the brain, his father in Dachau, a prisoner of Germany.

A few weeks later there was peace in Europe and we went back to Norway on one of the first cargo ships that took passengers. The captain was drunk all the time; once I saw him throw a kitten overboard.

In one cabin a blind man sat reading books by running his fingers over embossed paper. I was allowed to try it and can still remember the sensation in my fingertips.

Some naked cliffs provided the first impression of my country. They made Mamma cry and rush below to her cabin.

She was as old then as I am when I write this.

I tried for a long time to remember Papa. My pride in the new dress I had for the funeral and how everybody was kind and hugged me—that I remember.

But he himself—the man: there are so few pictures.

There was someone who once carried me up a flight of stairs and carefully laid me on a bed. My head rested in the hollow of his throat.

That must have been Papa.

A man walking with me along a country road. He was tall and wore a brown leather jacket and said nothing, but with our hands we made secret squeezing signals to each other.

That must have been Papa too.

My father, who was in my life for six years and did not leave me with one real memory of him. Just a great lack. That cut into me so deeply that many of life's experiences relate to it. The void Papa's death left in me became a kind of cavity, into which later experiences were to be laid.

In Trondhjem when I was small Mamma used to take me on her lap and tell me what a good time we had had in America. Showed me pictures of summer and children and parents standing with their arms round each other. Papa fishing and building a cooking place and latrine, while Mamma made garlands of flowers and hung them round our necks and waists instead of clothes. I was sorry because that time would never return.

We went to his grave every Sunday. Taking flowers or candles or a wreath. Mamma always looked sad. I hated standing in front of a cold white stone pretending it was Papa.

One day I buried all my dolls at his grave. I didn't want him to lie there alone. I stole flowers from other graves to brighten the place up for Papa and the dolls.

All the grownups were angry. And Mamma spoke about death so it became as beautiful for me as love.

I hoped I would die soon.

Linn, too, has a father who wears a brown leather jacket. One day when she is five I stand watching them. They are on a road together. A child's hand reaches in the air for his. She hasn't seen him for a whole year. A little girl with a face alight with trust and pride. Soon they will be standing hand in hand for all to see that she is out for a walk with her father.

But he is deep in conversation with another grownup and has forgotten the child at his side.

Slowly a hand is lowered, fiddles for a moment with some hair on her forehead. A distant look comes into the child's eyes. Our daughter locks herself into an experience. One that I, the bystander, recognize.

My first year at school I remember as long hours of sitting with apprehension in my stomach waiting for recess. Sometimes there were team games, but other breaks were endless minutes of lonely desperation during which I pretended to be busy with something I preferred to do alone.

Snowball fights in winter. The fear when the big boys forced my head down into the snow.

I was small and thin and wild. But I was the only one in the school who could do a handstand on the handlebars of a bicycle.

Once I circulated a paper on which I had written: "Liv's father was a drunk." I hoped the others would feel sorry for me and wonder who could be so dreadful as to write anything so mean.

Mamma often told my sister and me about the time when she was not alone, when she slept each night close by a man who loved her. A state of bliss which two daughters continued to fantasize about. Sometimes I heard her crying in the sitting room. That was strange and frightening. I thought that grownups were never afraid and indecisive. That they had their jobs and their parties and patted little children's heads. Bending down from their adult world, in which they had lived all their lives; looking at me with eyes that knew and understood everything. When I tiptoed in and tried to comfort Mamma, she pushed me away, telling me that I was too small, and that if I behaved, I would get something nice the next day.

I used to go to bed wearing one of my sister's dresses, hoping a prince would come during the night and carry me off.

And often I sat at the window looking for a man in a brown leather jacket.

The walk back from school. Girls huddled against an old brick wall. Tall trees, enabling us to imagine we lived in an enchanted castle which perhaps no one would ever come to free us from.

Whispered conversations about all that happened at night when we were asleep. Dead people who came back and touched the living. Suddenly appearing like pale ghosts one could never afterward forget.

There were dreams and thoughts I can no longer remember.

The first blue anemone. A slope suddenly covered with color where the previous day we had seen only grass. Clamber to the top and sit there hidden from the rest of the world and yet feeling a joyous part of it.

I know that I experienced something new on each bend of that school road which I can return to now in wonder because it seems so gray and without life.

Christmas is one of my best memories. Sitting in the cathedral with the organ notes reaching into every corner of the great building. On the way home we would freeze all the way along Munkegaten, which was still paved with cobbles. Other families to the right and left of us with the same happiness we felt.

Then home. And the smell of roast pork and pickled cabbage. The wait in a darkened room—where my sister and I sat on the floor, tingling inside, because we knew that in the sitting room a tree was being dressed for celebration. The rustle of paper and quick footsteps signaling secrets.

And when at last the door opened and we, who were children, saw the Christmas tree for the first time, standing in the middle of the floor, glittering with candles, we almost swooned with joy.

Mamma at the piano. She who was much younger than I realized. With longings I only now perceive when it is too late to share them.

Stories on the edge of the bed. Cocoa and bread and butter with bananas and apple jelly. A woman sitting bowed over a book, her head with short brown hair turned slightly away from me. Looking up now and then and smiling.

That was happiness.

I AM IN LOS ANGELES. TWENTY-FOUR HOURS AGO IN OSLO I trudged to the theatre in galoshes to play Nora in *A Doll's House*. Four days with no performances provides the opportunity to put the finishing touches to a film in Hollywood.

It was winter when I boarded the plane in Norway, and eighty degrees when I debarked twenty hours later in California.

I can't see the tops of the skyscrapers or the view from the hills because of the smog, which almost never lifts. If a person is found dead here, a postmortem will always reveal whether he has spent less than three weeks in the city. That is the length of time it takes this pollution to invade the body, after which it is there forever.

It is Sunday. I am lying in a hammock stretched between two palm trees. The cares and worries of the world don't penetrate here where there are roses and green lawns, faint music flowing from the open windows, where a friend gives me a cold drink—a mixture of juices of the fruits of the garden. It is a few hours' flight from reality. No telephones, no pressures. Peace.

I fall asleep there in the hammock and dream I am Nora, dancing a tarantella down Sunset Boulevard.

We are dining with friends. He is a director and has just finished his first important film. She is the wife who lives only for her husband's career. They lived for a number of years in New York, but have now moved to Los Angeles. Bought a house they cannot afford. Sought out company and the acquaintance of those they do not really care about. Maintained a social life with men and women with whom the only thing they have in common is the hope that the association can lead to future business.

For some it is lonely and impossible not to be in "the right circles," and they scramble and crawl over each other in order to be included; humiliate themselves and lose their souls somewhere on the way toward a goal that does not exist.

The director and his wife are having a difficult time. In her insecurity she strives so hard when they are with other people that she scares off those with whom she wishes contact. She tells them that her husband is the world's most talented man, that he will become the greatest of them all, make the best films, earn the most money—and any strength that he himself may lack, she will provide.

It is a year since I last saw her, and the change is striking. Then they had just arrived from New York, where they lived quite happily. She was perhaps a little plump and had lovely black hair, and was all eagerness over the life that awaited them in California. Now there are sharp little lines around her mouth. She is nervous and smokes all the time.

They talk enthusiastically about the parties they have been to, about all their plans and acquaintances. That she has lost twenty pounds—can you really recognize her?

Physically she is no longer as animated and alive. She looks defenseless and slightly pathetic. She has dyed her hair reddish and she talks on and on—as if not knowing what she is saying. I feel dreadfully sorry for her. She touches the protective instinct within me. She has such fine qualities, which will never blossom in the life they have now chosen. I believe she will be a different person each time I meet her. The impossible plans for the future she is building. Her longing for friendship, while she hunts useful connections. Loneliness beside the swimming pool and in their big new house with hardly any furniture. No children. Previously, they wanted to be just the two of them. Now they have the Career. The American dream. Success.

Her dream is to stand at her husband's side and be one of

the film city's influential people. Belong to the A group. She puts her arm through mine at table and we chat about nothing.

I feel her need of a woman friend—feel it in the gust of the confidences breathed into my ear.

The drinks are brought in. She smiles and encourages her husband. Tells us how clever he is, how good he is, how proud she is of him.

Fear sits at table with us—and I shudder at the thought of meeting her in ten years' time.

I WAS EIGHT AND MAMMA WAS GOING TO WORK IN A BOOK-store.

Then Karen came to us.

I don't know how old she was. But I remember that many ladies came to the house after Mamma placed an advertisement in the newspaper. They huddled together in an embarrassed group by the entrance. All of a sudden, one of them removed her hat and marched into the sitting room and sat down in the best chair. She smiled broadly, and the expression on her face said it was all settled.

That was Karen.

Mamma did not dare say no when Karen announced that she had decided to have the job the moment she saw "Madam."

I thought she was very fat and very ugly. And I loved her.

She was fond of her new little family—perhaps most of Mamma. It was as if she understood better than anyone what Mamma missed in her circle of married and well-to-do friends, and from the first day she placed Mamma on a pedestal. She took full charge without being asked to. Insisted that "Madam" should be free and able to relax when she came home from the bookstore.

Sometimes Karen took my sister and me out for walks. We were sure she did this so that people would think she was our mother. I was always afraid she might succeed. She wore such peculiar clothes and had a protruding jaw and moved in a clumsy way, and I always ran a little in front or behind her. No one was to suspect any relationship between us.

She used to take us with her into a dairy, where we had to drink milk still warm from the cow. It was horrid.

I remember Karen's smell. She was always baking bread

and washing the floor with borax soap. Her body was big and warm to lean against. One day she was in the kitchen crying because she had had all her teeth pulled. It took a whole week for the new set to be put in. She was suddenly a stranger because she had a peculiar hole in her face where her mouth had been. I avoided her as much as I could, and that made her cry all the more. With loud sniffs.

She was no good at reading stories, and she didn't even talk much. But when she made cocoa in the evenings and sat with us at the kitchen table and smiled just because *she,* too, was part of the family, I was as happy and secure as I ever remember being as a child.

Only once did we see Karen's home. We had gone for a Sunday walk and were passing the tall gray block of apartments where she lived. Mamma said we would pay her a surprise visit.

Karen's fright and uncertainty. A little dark room with a hot plate and dishes and toilet things piled on the single table. Newspapers on the chairs, one window looking onto a white wall only a few feet away. A narrow bed—I wondered how Karen's fat body could get any rest on it.

She gave us coffee and Mamma did all the talking. Karen looked relieved when we had to go.

"That will have made Karen happy," Mamma said.

We often experience things in different ways.

She died in her sleep one night in that narrow bed. I cried much more than when Mamma told me Papa was dead.

It pricks my conscience when I think that perhaps she understood why I always ran in front of her, or behind, on the street.

IT'S A WORKING DAY IN HOLLYWOOD. I AM HERE TO RECORD twenty lines for a film soon to have its premiere.

The producer is in a corner of the studio tending a heavy hangover. The director is in his place. Seven technicians sit silent behind a sheet of glass. The room is full of microphones and wires.

This is Jan Troell's first American film. He stands in the middle of the floor, swinging his powerful arms to and fro in deliberate sweeping motions. One hand grasps an invisible racket. In the evening he is to be coached by an ex–world champion of tennis. Swing your arms—stand up a little on your toes—bend your back—and serve! No one is surprised at his somewhat unusual behavior.

The producer remains immobile throughout the morning. He has a red beard, which does not suit him, and kind eyes. He is deep in a golden dream. The film we are working on is either his arrival or his exit as producer. If it turns out well, he will be able to pay for his house, install his own tennis court, get money for another film, sign up the actors he wants. His modest appearance will no longer be a hindrance.

I have a thousand things on my mind—everything I must do before I fly home to Oslo and the theatre.

And while we are, to all appearances, taken up with entirely different things, a movie has acquired twenty new lines.

Quite a few people have gathered for lunch. New film projects are discussed. Success is measured by the number of offers one receives. The more money you are offered, the more producers ring your agent and offer yet more.

This is Hollywood's way of talking about the weather.

An elderly actor stops at our table. He is German. A flood

of words at furious speed: his wife has left him and their five children. He whispers, looking around nervously, hinting that I am the only one to receive this confidence. But I can hear that he has told his story many times. To all who have time to listen.

He can't understand. Had thought they were so happy. She had the lovely house. Its location was a bit isolated—he would admit that—but it was so beautiful . . . and, after all, she was never alone, plenty to do with the children. He was always good to her, in love with her, did everything he could to see that she was happy. Perhaps he was away traveling too much, but when he couldn't get work in the film city itself— what was he to do?

Now she had gone, and he tells me confidentially he is sure she was crazy all along. Only he had never realized it. He had been too gullible. He was going to get a doctor's certificate of insanity so that she could never come back with claims on the children. Would I give evidence in court?

He is thin and his hands tremble. Once he was a handsome man that many a girl tried to get. And eventually he wed the youngest of them all. There were children—one every year— and they both waited for happiness to follow. Something in which to relax and feel secure. Now the two will meet in court. And everything they didn't know about each other they will reveal to indifferent and tired attorneys.

EVERY SATURDAY I ARRANGED A THEATRICAL PERFORMANCE in the school gym. Writing the script myself, directing it myself and taking the best parts. After the first few performances, I was so ill-prepared, the cast had to improvise in front of the audience. As a result, my productions became poorly attended.

But that didn't matter. What did we want an audience for?

We lived off our own pleasure: the make-up, the costumes, the endless possibility for fantasy. Never since has the theatre been such fun. Never again will I achieve the same contact with the written word. The laughter and the tears; the solidarity with the others, who were also living out their secret lives on the bare boards of the gym.

The magical moment when I was a little girl and Thalia for the first time showed me her two faces.

The movies on allowance day. Queues winding round corners, making the feast inside even more fantastic because access to it was so difficult.

I no longer remember everything I saw, but the emotions, the excitement, the smell are still vivid. The sound of a bell, the light slowly dimming. Eyes tight shut, the more so for the hands pressed against them; and when finally you looked again, the miracle was already there on the screen.

The pictures, the flight from reality, the world of dreams: experiences and people I believed would become part of my everyday life in the future. Tragedies so great that there was still a lump in the throat many hours later. Wonders so great that my feet did not touch the ground all the way home.

Miracle in Milan. Limelight. I saw them ten or twenty

times, and the enchantment was just as real each time. Heroes and Heroines. People who were either Good or Evil. Almost never ordinary and boring like the people I knew in Trondhjem.

And Love.

I yearned to experience it as it happened on the screen: stand close up against a man with a white shirt and a white smile who looked down at me tenderly and whispered the same words the Hero was whispering to the Heroine.

Hear violins when he kissed me.

If only I could grow up a little quicker. I cast an anxious glance at my flat breasts.

ON THE WAY BACK FROM LOS ANGELES TO NORWAY WE have a two-hour stopover at London airport. I have an important meeting with a friend, a very gifted writer.

I am a privileged first-class passenger, allowed to use a small lounge, sink into soft cushions, be served free drinks accompanied by muted music.

We talk about a film we want to make together. He has been working on the script for several months. It is Karen Blixen's story that has captured our imagination. A woman who, as Isak Dinesen, wrote down her account of a love affair with a country and so created one of the literary masterpieces of our age. I see the project as a way of getting close to her. Read about her, talk with people who had met her, get into her books again. Visit her beloved Africa. I will spend a year of my life delving into her world.

I am sure this is something I want to do. Even if my agent says no, because perhaps the idea is uncommercial. The time has passed when the mere making of a film was an adventure in itself. When I uncritically said yes to everything. I am sitting with a man who doesn't speak of money or promise that my name will come before the title of the film. (That, of course, is the grandest of all—something many will take less salary to achieve.) My friend wants me to do it not just because of what he sees in me as an actress, but also because of what he sees in me as a woman.

I tell him that I will gladly make the film for nothing.

Flight time.

Away from the first-class lounge, writers, plans for the future, Hollywood. I am on my way to Norway. To the theatre and the evening's performance.

I am happy.

I look forward to the sense of freedom that comes in the silence and the laughter from the audience. It is in that contact I get my reward—much more than in the applause afterward.

Long narrow corridors and dressing rooms that are small and overcrowded. The joy of working in a team. The smell of old furniture and stage sets. Recognizing well-used costumes now hanging up waiting, freshly ironed. Living the life that was mine when almost no one knew I existed there.

FEAR OF THE DARK.

I was twelve. My sister, two years older than I, made her first sorties into social life, and Mamma had an active circle of friends. I was too old to have a baby-sitter.

The whole day I was filled with this: fear of the moment when the last one called "Good night" from the hall and I, lying in bed, heard the door bang shut. The apartment that thundered at me with its stillness.

The dark corners. The pounding heart. Papa's photograph under my pillow. A bowl of water on the bedside table so that I could be continually wetting my eyes to keep them open. The danger of falling asleep and being attacked by something hiding among the terrors of the night.

Finally, the escape into the bathroom. The relief when the door could be locked. A room where I had every corner in full view. A quilt and books as security. An exhausted sleep on the bathroom floor until the first one came home and hammered on the door and asked what kind of childish nonsense was going on.

A TAXI LINE AFTER A PERFORMANCE OF *A Doll's House* IN Oslo. There is luggage because I have just returned today from abroad. It is half-past eleven and I am weary. A working day in Hollywood followed by a twenty-hour flight and a three-hour performance. People in the line stare at me, because they have just been in the theatre and seen me in costume. I am not looking my best now and glower back at them from where I sit on one of my suitcases. The applause and the cheers are left behind in the seats and on the stage. Now the public and the actress are shy and wary of each other.

In the taxi I pretend to be asleep to avoid talking with the driver, answering the questions: Isn't it exciting to travel so much, fun to act, and haven't I become very rich?

Only when the driver has dropped me outside my house do I discover that I have forgotten the key. Linn is not home and I see myself spending the night on the steps with my luggage. A modern "Little Match Girl" dying in the winter's cold with checkbook and jewelry in her suitcase.

My neighbor has a spare key. I walk the few yards to her door. A laughing face at the window when I ring the bell—then another: her husband's. She comes to the door, smiles and chatters as if I had not disturbed them in the middle of the night. She is wearing a short little nightie with a pattern of flowers. Her legs are bare and pretty, and she keeps hopping up and down because of the cold.

I get my key; her husband taps on the window and waves. She comes up behind him and puts her arms round his neck. Perhaps I arrived just as they were making love.

Let myself into my own home and lie down on the bed. Feel that I am excluded from something that is vital. The fear inside of loneliness: That only what others have is *real*.

DANCING SCHOOL. THIRTEEN YEARS OLD. SKINNY AND UN-gainly, with close-cropped hair.

The tunes of those days still fill me with aversion. A memory of boys in white shirts storming across the floor when the mistress clapped her hands and said, "Take partners."

Always the same little group who pretended to be thinking of something else when they sat down and the dance began without them. And the next dance, when they had to stand up and the boys crossing the floor at a snail's pace were made to take one of them first.

The wallflowers of my generation.

Who never realized that they shared the fate of thousands of women, small and grown up, all over the world. Thirteen-year-olds convinced they would remain wallflowers for the rest of their lives. For each, an experience that seemed unique.

The teacher petite and elegant. Dancing around as if finding a rhythm was the easiest thing in the world, as much a part of her as the piled-up hair with small curls and the stiletto heels on her shoes. She had dresses that were always new and pretty, jewelry glittering from ears, neck and fingers. The breasts and small waist above the curve of the hips and the long red nails put a definite end to a thirteen-year-old's feeling of self-worth.

The anxiety during intermissions.

Going home, when it seemed that everyone else went off in groups or couples. A foretaste of the woman's feeling of abandonment when *she* is alone, and it is Sunday, and everything around her lives and breathes of togetherness and family.

The first ball spent in the ladies' room wearing my sister's discarded pink silk dress.

I accepted my failure as understandable and complete.

Envisioned spending the rest of my life as an outsider. But preferably behind a closed door, so that no one would know.

EVERY DAY I TRY TO WRITE. IT IS MOST DIFFICULT AT HOME, where there are telephone calls, Linn, nursemaids, neighbors. If I had been a man it would have been different. A man's profession is respected much more, as is the work he does at home, his fatigue, his need to concentrate.

Try telling a child that *Mamma* is working, when the child can see with its own eyes that she is just sitting there writing. Explain to the nurse you pay dearly to do what is expected of you—explain that this is important, is supposed to be finished by a certain date—and off she goes, shaking her head, convinced I am neglecting my child and my home. Success in one's profession and trying to write a book do not compensate for domestic shortcomings as obvious as mine.

I sit in the basement hammering on my typewriter. Until bad conscience drives me up to the kitchen. I have coffee with the maid, read to Linn, and am polite on the telephone as if I had all the time in the world.

But the whole time I am seething with anger. It is astonishing that so much anger can be contained behind such a mild façade.

Calls from America, and from Paris and England and Oslo. Only one is a call I hope for, which is what forces me to take them all. The nurse never answers the telephone—she can't speak English.

My publisher suggests that I unplug the instrument. But my phone rings just the same, because it was wrongly installed. I can put the thing in a closet, but the wall rings. It is quite difficult to write under such conditions.

I run to the telephone, I talk to California, where it is night—how soft and strange the air there. Here the sun is shining—snow on the spruces outside my window. I sit in one world and talk with another. I doodle on a piece of paper and my conscience bothers me. Because I am a bad mother, because I am inadequate, don't answer letters, don't mend the faucets but allow them to go on dripping for months on end.

I have coffee with a neighbor and make excuses for everything I am doing, because I know that she will never understand why this is important for me. This terrible "female guilt." I dare not have music on when I am in the basement, writing, lest upstairs they think I am just sitting here loafing. I feel that to be respected I must produce pancakes and home-baked bread and have neat, tidy rooms.

These are my thoughts as I try to write about how good it is to have a life that gives so much freedom, so many choices: "I can be free by my own will, be my own creator and guide. My growth and my development depend on what I choose or discard in life. In me are the seeds of my future life."

The telephone rings. The maid knocks on the door and enters before I have time to respond. She has discovered a hole in Linn's pants.

I laugh into the telephone, and afterward discuss at length whether to darn the hole or sew on a patch of some gay material.

SCHOOL.

Subjects, lessons—I have more or less forgotten what they were. Everything that I even then felt was of no use for my later life is relegated to the back of my memory, where all wasted time, all blunders, all stupidities form a hard little lump which periodically I can reach back and feel.

It is easier for me to recall visual impressions: the color of the teachers' desks, of different shapes and sizes, standing threateningly at the end of the classrooms, with long brown pointers lying across them. Chalk, which either broke in the hand or made unpleasant squeaks on the blackboard.

The woolen gloves we had to make in sewing class, gym trousers and school aprons which became dirtier and dirtier between my sweating, reluctant fingers. Rivers and boundaries and mountain ranges I learned by heart in endless rigmaroles—glibly recited one day and totally forgotten the next.

School cooking lessons: polishing the stoves, beating warm blood for black pudding, and scrubbing the floor. A teacher so full of fury that I never regretted my alternative solution of pouring boiling water over my foot so that I could spend the lesson in the hospital instead. Constant admonishments: "You can't think with your head on your arms" (as a grownup I have always thought better with my head on my arms); "You'll become a cripple if you sit with your legs crossed" (as a grownup I double-cross my legs).

In the end I detested school so much that I was continually playing truant; I stayed at home, thinking that I had persuaded Mamma that my cold or stomachache was real. Until one day she strode into my bedroom with a child psychologist and a nurse. While Mamma wept in the background, the nurse dressed me and the psychologist talked a lot of nonsense in a gentle voice and drove me to the hospital.

There, in a large ward with children who really were ill—
heart ailments, brain operations and a squalling infant—I lay
on public display as a truant. Tormented by the nurses' con-
tempt for my pink-cheeked health, I one day jumped out of
the window and ran around the garden in my pajamas, embraced a meditating doctor in a white coat and asked him with
tears in my eyes if he would be my father. This moving performance had an immediate effect: I was placed in a single
room and considered to be truly ill. The whole class wrote me
letters, and Mamma sat beside the bed with a worried look in
her eyes, and the child psychologist asked if I understood that
everybody only wanted the best for me. And the school—the
whole school—missed me, and Mamma missed me, and my
sister missed me, and did I understand that I had worried
them all? And when I said that I understood that, the psychologist told Mamma he had cured me, and to me he said
that now I could return home and be nice to Mamma and
work hard at school. I took his hand and curtsied nicely and
put on my gentlest smile while I thanked him for all he had
done for me. Especially for coming into my bedroom without
warning and shoving me into the hospital.

Later I decided I was going to become a child prodigy, just
to show him. Write a book the whole world would marvel at.
It was to be very sad, and everyone would wonder how such a
young girl could write such a profound and melancholy book.

One of the teachers at my elementary school I remember
with great pleasure, and later another in high school. There
were others, of course, but with these two I was in close and
wordless contact. The former wrote at the bottom of one of
my compositions: "Dear Liv, you have great imagination and
an unusual ability to express it. But sometimes you get into
deep water—and it's a long swim to land from there. This,
too, is an image. Do you understand, little Liv, what I mean?"

Little Liv understood, and she kept his letter until she had grown up.

And there was another teacher with red cheeks and black-rimmed spectacles. Without him, high school would have been as meaningless as my hopelessly dirty school apron.

I was short and thin and quite self-centered, lost in daydreams. Good reports and enormous boredom. My breasts were at times Mamma's gloves stuffed into a secret bra bought with saved-up allowance. Gym classes, which most girls missed once a month by saying "usual reason" in a matter-of-fact voice when their names were called out. And when it never happened to me, I pretended it had, but I could never keep track of the dates. For a whole year I was a fraud—without realizing that all the others *knew,* only the teacher had asked them to be tactful and pretend they didn't.

"Usual reason": the magical expression that distinguishes the initiated from the others. And then the time finally comes. What joy! What agony! Lucky woman, when the first trace of blood takes her from the land of innocence and into the world that will become for her more and more mysterious.

With her savings she bought artist's materials, an easel and exciting tubes of oil paints. Watched without envy her girlfriends' romantic dates; she, herself, was going to become a world-famous artist.

And, later, a journalist. She published newspapers. Wrote plays and poetry. At one period she wanted to become a veterinarian. Have a big house, fill it with homeless cats and dogs; all of them would lie on large silk cushions.

But most of all, and finally, she wanted to be an actress.

I am certain that there were times when I was the leader of my class, but what I remember best is being the "outsider," the sense of being different.

What I recollect is that which went deepest—and for me the sense of isolation was the traumatic experience.

Lying in bed at night listening to the grownups laughing and talking in the sitting room, thinking, When I grow up I will be part of this wonderful world of ideas and laughter.

But I have grown up, and at times still feel the outsider, believing that everyone else is part of some togetherness.

I forget how real they are, those childhood experiences which we grownups call fantasy.

To the child it isn't fantasy: the fear of being abandoned, the wicked wolf, the darkness in the closet—it is all *real*. One puts a name on it in order to call it something else.

What is real we say is a fantasy—and *that* is the fantasy.

I AM IN PARIS FOR THREE DAYS. IT IS NOT MY FIRST TIME, and the circumstances of my earlier visits have always been a little odd.

When I was quite young I came with a Norwegian theatre company. I was unhappily in love and only wanted to lie on my bed and read old letters from *him*. He went on a walking tour in the mountains to forget me. He ran up and down and around all the peaks he could find, timed himself, beat his own records, and after a while couldn't remember why he had begun running. While I dragged myself to Sarah Bernhardt's old theatre and acted out my suffering on the stage.

I didn't even bother to see the Eiffel Tower.

The next time I came here was to take the final scenes of a film I had made in the south of France. We worked at a little damp studio from eight in the morning until late in the evening. Almost everyone around me spoke French, which I didn't understand. My co-actor, Charles Bronson, who didn't know French either, was not much comfort. Throughout the whole time he scarcely spoke to me. "Good morning" and "Goodbye" and "I'm not looking forward to working with you again"—at least that's what he appeared to be saying. Already he was one of Europe's biggest box-office stars, and it might have been depressing for him to work with someone from little Norway. Fame came to him late in life, and now he spent the day exercising his big arm muscles, clenching and unclenching his fists, inflating and deflating his chest, while sweat decorated his upper lip.

I didn't see the Eiffel Tower this time either.

On my third visit I was accompanied by my five-year-old daughter and her nurse. I was filming in London when the nurse's fiancé started to write cold letters. He didn't like his woman being out of the country. As a result she had dark circles under her eyes and was anything but gay. I invited her for a weekend in Paris in order to cheer her up.

Three girls on a spree: Linn, who had just learned English and was now bewildered by French, the nurse, who was receiving the cold letters, and myself, weary after a week's strenuous work. Put to the vote, there was little enthusiasm for the Louvre and Notre Dame, and we went to stores and toy shops. I smiled to my child and I smiled to the nurse—while protesting inside.

When eventually we reached the Eiffel Tower I was exhausted and dizzy. I just couldn't go up with them, so I sat on a seat and froze and waited.

And now I am here for the fourth time, to give interviews to newspapers and television and radio. Both *Cries and Whispers* and *The Emigrants* are attracting full houses.

By day I see only the hotel room. The schedule is full from early morning until late in the evening. My sister, who has come with me, is the only one who makes any use of the car and chauffeur placed at my disposal.

But not even she sees more than the big stores. Her conscience is bothering her because of a family left at home. She is afraid her husband and the five children won't be able to manage without her. She buys presents to give them when she returns.

A press agent has decided in advance how long each interview is to last: *France-Soir, L'Express, Le Monde, Elle, Paris Match*. Breakfast and lunch and dinner with questions and answers. Coffee with television, supper with radio. Journalists meet each other on their way in and out. Look suspicious at the sight of a colleague. As if I am in possession of secrets they want for themselves alone. If I have to go to the bathroom, it causes panic: I am robbing someone of his time. They are waiting there in the sitting room with their pencils and tape recorders.

And soon the next one will be knocking on the door.

Most of them want to know the same things, but they phrase their questions differently. I vary my answers as best I can to keep my poor press agent awake. He stands for hours by the window following the path of the sun, boredom painted on his face.

Do I believe in marriage? What is it like working with Ingmar Bergman? Do I have political interests? Am I a good mother? Do I live alone? What do I wish to make of my profession? They almost all ask what my attitude is to Women's Lib. I try to put into words why I believe that all division of people into groups just increases our difficulties. Makes it harder for us to understand one another.

I believe we can easily overemphasize our differences. Insisting on them is merely to classify what has already been classified to everyone's detriment.

I shudder to think what would have happened to the child Mozart if he had been a child today.

My sister, Bitten, and I are curious about night life in Paris. We want to see all the things we can't find at home. I have friends: Frenchmen who delight in showing off their capital.

We absorb smells . . . sights . . . colors. Sit at a long table in a dimly lit restaurant, eating and drinking. The proximity of strangers, the warmth of other people's bodies, all of us squeezed close against each other.

There is a show on a tiny stage. Fifty women and men

clowning uninhibitedly. Running in and out in fantastic costumes. Perspiring faces in continually different make-up. A
profusion of speed and elegance and light and confetti and
humor. Fantasy blossoms and captures us. My sister forgets
her bad conscience. Eyes shining, she is at her most beautiful.
People look at her and must be thinking that Nordic women
are the loveliest. I wish her husband were here. This is something for them to share.

The master of ceremonies recognizes me, and I am shoved
up onto the stage, have the arc lights turned on me. For a moment, I am aware of a warmth, experience admiration in
snatches of words I understand. For a moment I am joyously
proud and intoxicated with success. Then the photographers
arrive. Tipsy men make me write something on a menu or on
their arm. Mothers thrust bits of paper at me that I am to sign
for their children. I become embarrassed in front of my
friends. Bashfulness makes my feet and hands grow until they
are yards long. Soon everyone will notice I have a safety pin
in my dress, that I have a broken nail. They will find out I am
less than pretty, not at all amusing or remarkable.

We hurry away.

Dark little bars and people different from us. A man dances
with himself in front of a large mirror. He is in another
world—smiles and curtsies and throws kisses to his own reflec-
tion. Now and then he strokes his abdomen and tries to
seduce himself. Men dance with men, showing each other
tenderness, caressing each other. In the darkness, smoke and
loud music, people meet and part. We can see the need to
touch. We feel the need to touch.

See me. Love me.

It is early morning. We walk along the river. We can smell
spring, feel it against our skin. Little shops that are open

around the clock. We rummage on dusty shelves. Buy memories for each other. Scrawl greetings that have meaning only for these moments. Holding each other's hands, light-hearted after a long night together and smiling to everyone we meet. And at this time of day greetings are always returned.

Then back to the hotel. A quick shower. We stuff our things into suitcases. Collapse on the bed laughing because it feels lovely to be two sisters in the world together.

We are in high spirits on our way to the airport. The press agent looks at us with a weary and uncomprehending gaze. He runs down long corridors with our luggage, because we are too late to check it in. He runs ahead of us with the heavy suitcases, which he won't allow us to carry ourselves and he seems relieved as he kisses our hands and says he hopes we shall soon meet again.

Then, all at once, we are in Oslo. The start of another working day. It is twelve noon. Quickly I say goodbye to Bitten and rush off. She seems short of sleep, and happy, and is looking forward to getting home with her presents and everything she has to tell. Home to the reality that is hers.

And I run on—to a reality I do not always acknowledge.

Mamma contracted tuberculosis. Every Sunday Bitten and I went to the sanatorium and waved. She looked like a stranger, we thought. For the first time I became aware of her as a human being with a reality beyond that of being my mamma. I missed her during the six months she was away and put her picture under my pillow instead of Papa's. When she came back, she was much heavier and no longer as young. She had more time than before. And I less for her.

I was in love for the first time. Although I didn't hear bells ringing, as Mamma had promised me. But it was wonderful even so.

His name was Jens.

We didn't talk much, for we were both shy—silence was part of our relationship. Life pulsated around us differently than it had earlier. Our good-nights by the gate were tremendously important. The nearest we ever came to bells ringing. Mamma began standing at the window behind the curtains when she expected me home. We had to find other gates. He almost always wore rubber boots and was much taller than I. One day he told me that it was over. He could not spend all his youth with a virgin, he said. Somewhere he had read that it might be harmful for a developing man not to have sex. Besides, he was about to take his exams and go to the university. As a student he could not go around with a fifteen-year-old. He hoped I understood and wouldn't take it personally.

We both had red faces. I had never heard him speak that many consecutive sentences. I stood by a strange gate carrying my innocence with shame, as I watched a gangling youth walk out of my life.

For several months after this I loved James Stewart. He was the standby of my youth, uncomplicated, always there to love when needed. When, much later, I met him in person, I blushed furiously. As if he could guess the adventures the two of us shared in my dreams.

When there was an interval in the passions, I attended a sewing circle. We kept together for many years. Confidences whispered over a bottle of soda, which later was replaced by cocoa, then tea, and in the end by Coca-Cola with aspirin in it. Young girls on the threshold of life, who would meet by chance in the street many years later. Evaluating and curious, they would observe the changes in each other.

Walks around the harbor. Sunlight and air off the sea. Boats and fishermen and the atmosphere of a life utterly different from mine. The picture gallery in Trondhjem. Hours spent making the acquaintance of old masters and contemplating whether, after all, it wasn't an artist I ought to be. Each afternoon find a corner of Mamma's bookstore and sit there and read in the semidarkness. Search the rows of shelves. Sniff the lovely smell of paper and printer's ink.

Books have always been living things to me. Some of my encounters with new authors have changed my life a little. When I have been perplexed, looking for something I could not define to myself, a certain book has turned up, approached me as a friend would. And between its covers carried the questions and the answers I was looking for.

I was a member of the YWCA. A great woman, Sophie, allowed young girls to explore their literary and artistic interests. I was permitted to stage plays I had written myself. Read poetry to the old ladies who were members there. A memory of graying hair and gentle eyes. Hands cupped round the ears in order to hear better. Hymns and coffee. We often talked about God and to God. But never in a dogmatic way. I never noticed any intolerance. I know that I used to stand outside rubbing off my lipstick before I went in, but I believe that was due to my own wish to please.

One day I inadvertently went into a room where Sophie was kneeling on the floor, praying. She was in tears. I thought it would be difficult and embarrassing to meet her afterward, but she just smiled to me and patted my cheek.

Many years later she was standing outside my theatre in Oslo. She looked much smaller and appeared shy and embarrassed. A car was waiting for me and we stood there awkwardly, not knowing what to say to each other.

I didn't tell her that she had given me some of the most precious hours of my youth. I forgot to ask for her address before she hurried away.

Sophie saying thank you for the performance—the actress on her way to a cocktail party.

HOME FROM A TRIP. I HAVEN'T TIME TO WAIT FOR MY luggage, and I pay a porter to send it on when it comes. Fling myself into a taxi. There is a rehearsal at the theatre. My head is throbbing with weariness. I arrive at a run, a quarter of an hour late. Smile to right and left. Afraid of inconveniencing my colleagues. Afraid they may think me vain because I was in Paris being made much of. I forget they don't know the life I've just left. Here in Norway it is as if all that does not exist. Without any transition, I slip back into what is Oslo and the theatre. The other is already a dream.

The rehearsal over, I run on. Swedish television is waiting in a restaurant. They are to make a program with me the following week. On the way I stop to phone home. A small child cries and wonders where I am. Pangs of conscience seize me. Promise presents and things I'll do. The crying stops at the other end.

My meeting with the television people is disposed of in an hour. I rush on. My lawyer needs a signature on various papers. I buy presents for Linn. Phone home again. Notice that the tone of the baby-sitter's voice is rather cool. Back to the theatre. Sit under the hair dryer, trying to concentrate on the evening's performance. Constant phone calls. I hate that little black apparatus! A photographer has managed to get past the porter and is suddenly there in the doorway. "Just wanted a picture," he says. A man has painted a portrait of me from a photograph and insists that he be allowed to come to my dressing room to see if the colors are mine. Someone has sent me a poem he has written: surely we can meet and talk about it for five minutes? I don't have five minutes. Scripts lie unread on my dressing table. I have promised to give my reactions by a certain date and have no idea of what I should say.

Tears aren't far away. I cover myself with Nora's red cheeks and happy mouth. Look into the mirror: am both sad and happy.

A full house. Applause and flowers.

Hurried goodbyes in the elevator. My luggage, sent from the airport, is waiting for me in the doorkeeper's lodge. No press agent now to carry it for me. A taxi home. The babysitter asleep on the sofa. I wake her, and, in the mood to chat, she stays on for three-quarters of an hour. I have no idea what we say to each other. There has been a telephone call from one of the Famous. He's in all the papers today. His widely publicized marriage had been canceled the day before the wedding. The bride got cold feet, they report. I am sure he phoned me to tell me what a relief it was that nothing came of it. He would have laughed his high laugh and asked if he might come and visit me in Oslo. Hoping that we could be seen together in public, show the papers and people that he wasn't alone. I know he is having a difficult time, but I just can't ring him back. This night I haven't the strength to pretend I don't hear his desperation.

A price is paid for fame. I remember when Kissinger was given the Nobel Prize. I sent him a telegram from a little village in Italy, hoping it would reach him through all the festivities. A few hours later he rang to thank me. His voice did not sound especially happy and there were no sounds of celebration in the background.

A journalist once asked me how it felt to have been given so many prizes and honors.

"Unfortunately, I'm afraid I can't converse with them," I said.

He laughed and thought I was being funny.

No.

I am here in a house too big for Linn and me. I am sad and tired and pleased. But I have no one I can share it with.

In my bed is a little girl. She barely wakes as I lie down close to her.

"Mamma, my mouth is full of kisses."

IT WAS THE YEAR THEY PLAYED "MOONLIGHT SERENADE" on the radio. The year we saw the film about Glenn Miller and wept over his tragic death. Rock was introduced in Norway. All the girls wore wide skirts with several layers of starched petticoats underneath. The year when one was constantly falling in love. Body and soul were full of fragrance and happiness. I had come to terms with school, because I no longer cared about it. My reports were good, but I regarded the school subjects as useless for later life.

We still had no television. The rest of the world did not seem so close as it does today. We strolled along Nordre Gate and longed for the Great Love. To be on the safe side and make sure of not missing it, I made several dates for the same evening; Mamma and various girlfriends were sent to the designated street corners to tell the waiting young men that I wasn't well.

Few of us defied the morals we were taught at home. Seldom have there been so many reluctant virgins of seventeen as the year they introduced kissproof lipstick. We boasted of experiences we did not have. Whispered our longings to those closest to us. Girls of my generation dreamed of freedom and a profession. But we also had a burning desire to be married and taken care of.

Women's Lib didn't reach Trondhjem in my day.

No! THIS WON'T DO! THIS WILL NEVER BE A BOOK. WHERE
on earth can I go to be left in peace? Just one hour's peace.
Mostly I long to do nothing. To lie stretched out on my
bed and be brought lovely food and be taken care of by
kind people. Who look at me with worried expressions and
say that I'm working far too hard. I am. Normal people
don't rush about the world the way I do. Last March I made
three trips to Los Angeles while playing in Ibsen's *Brand* at
the Norwegian Theatre and starting an American film in
Sweden.

This spring is no better. I shall never learn to say no. I
dread it every time the telephone rings: is it my publisher, to
scold me because he hasn't yet seen any typescript; or my
agent sitting on his backside in California wondering what on
earth I am playing at here in Norway; or the theatre director
phoning to say that I am to go on tour with *A Doll's House*?
And then there is Linn and mother and sister and friends and
this and that and I'm so tired I just want to sit down and
scream.

But they would think I am mad. They don't understand
how it feels never to be able to heave a sigh of relief at the
thought that tomorrow is Sunday and a day of rest.

Day of rest?

I rush to the damned typewriter every free hour I have. All
because two years ago a journalist rang me up when I was out
of work and asked what I was doing. And instead of admitting
I had nothing and producing a headline: "THE END OF A
CAREER," I chose to say that I was writing a book.

Everybody asks about the book. Publishers phone or write
from all over the world without any idea of what I am sitting
here shoveling together. Now I am just afraid. Terrified of

this contract that must be fulfilled. Scared of the half-promises I have given.

But I am going to fool them: get an enormous advance and run off to a peaceful island nobody knows about. Sit there and eat bananas and never come back.

The more I think of it, the more certain I am that the root of all my worries and all my fatigue is the *book,* and my promise to the Norwegian publisher that I will deliver a manuscript by a certain date.

Aha! The publisher is the villain.

My old friend! Well, I no longer know about that. I need him more as a scapegoat. With trembling, angry fingers I dial his number. I must be mad.

"Mamma," Linn says.

"Shut up," I hiss, and so that she will never forget it, add: "Men—throw them out."

"Men are God's creatures too," says my little child, and walks out into the sun.

It is difficult to explain over the telephone what I have on my mind; but he understands it is something that can't wait. Speaks to me as if I were an animal with which one can't deal rationally. We agree to meet at once.

I don't put on any make-up. Am glad to see that my nose is shiny and that there are black shadows under my eyes. For a moment I wonder whether Camille wouldn't make a deeper impression on him than The Monster. I elect to go for something in between and set out in the worn trousers I garden in. Laugh an exaggerated laugh to myself when people look at me as if they understood why I am on the list of the world's worst-dressed women. If they think the *outside* awful, they should just see what I'm like inside.

It's ten miles into Oslo. The Monster gives way more and more to Camille. I am at the edge of tears. Sit in the car, long for him to understand. Picture him getting up and putting his arms around me for comfort. Moving his chair up to mine and whispering into my ear that first and foremost he is my friend. That I mustn't worry. That he understands. That everything is all right. He can publish some other books, anything, as long as I am happy.

I get to our meeting place and find that he has ordered cocoa and cream for me. He has already had a shrimp sandwich, and there's a bit of mayonnaise at the corner of his mouth. I drop my gaze, stare into the cup and blink to keep back the tears. I know that I can never explain convincingly. I wish it were not so vague even to me. Just a big lump in my midriff. I can no longer stand the pressure of all the demands.

Fear of being left empty-handed after having revealed myself. Doubt about the contents of this book and whether it will reach others.

As I look up at him, stammering bad arguments, trying to explain that there can never be a book, the *friend* slowly fades. In his place is the *employer,* someone I don't know. I expect horns to grow out of his forehead. I don't believe I have ever met such a heartless man. Just because I am a single woman!

I am going to become a militant feminist and fight him and his kind. The next time he shows me his writing cottage (he is an author too), where he works every morning and afternoon undisturbed by children or the telephone, I shall say something really nasty and cutting.

And all the while as I drink my cocoa and cream (he orders a second one) and spill a little on the table (my hands are shaking) and promise to spend more of my time writing (what time?), I am thinking of all the money he is going to make on me.

Never has so abused a martyr looked so sorrowfully at her oppressor before stumbling out and home.

In the car I wonder if I am having a nervous breakdown. And if so, can I give it artistic expression?

I CAN CERTAINLY UNDERSTAND THAT VARIOUS MEMBERS OF Papa's family looked askance at my choice of profession. To bear the name Ullmann has its obligations, or so I was told as a child. You have to maintain certain standards, have a motto for your life—a fenced road to one's goal, based on the best traditions. One of the older members of the family wrote to Mamma saying that perhaps it was best that Papa had died before his daughter became ensnared by the stage.

I was not invited to many of the family gatherings. During my first year in Oslo I occasionally ran into one or another of the Ullmanns in the street. But all the time they were looking at me with rather frightened eyes I felt, nonetheless, that deep down there was some contact. If only we gave each other time to understand and accept. We were of the same roots; it was just that we had grown in slightly different directions.

Great-grandfather is the one the family is most proud of. His name was Viggo Ullmann, a liberal and president of the Parliament and founder of a new kind of school. He was known to be a great speaker. An extremely ugly man, as are almost all Ullmanns. Both the religious ones and the atheists. There God makes no distinction, no superficial rewards for good behavior.

"I believe in eternal life, because I am living it," my grandfather used to say. In his day, the ladies of the family used their eternal life to work for the freedom of women. Most of them were educators. The Norwegian author Gunnar Heiberg wrote a play, *Aunt Ulrikke,* about one of them. Her true name was Aasta Hansteen and she was angry and able, hated men and was full of humor. Then there was a relative who was slightly crazy. At a mature age he ran away with a traveling theatrical company. No one heard from him thereafter, nor was his name ever mentioned. It is he, I suppose, that I take after.

At the premiere of my first film, *Young Escape,* one of my great-uncles went to the director of the Oslo Cinemas and asked if anything could be done to stop its being shown. In the film I bathed naked in a forest lake and the Ullmann behind was clearly visible for all to see.

The film was reported to the police by a certain Pastor Moll, who made a habit of reporting nakedness whenever he encountered it—whether in sculpture or in a newspaper account of a naked dancer.

Family scandal.

Grandma ran into difficulties at her old-people's home, because she had invited all the ladies in her corridor to the premiere. Things did not improve for her when I sent a poem to a magazine, signing her name, and they returned it to her with a note stating it was too erotic.

Once I went to a party given by Papa's cousin. I was married then, and had just had an artistic success in the capital and for the first time was an honored guest at a family party. In his little speech of welcome, my host confessed to the greatest sin he had committed: the theft of jam from his mother's pantry when he was five. Presumably it still tormented him. This made me understand better why he might feel I was immoral.

Mamma's family is not as dignified as Papa's. In my childhood I was much closer to them, because I lived in the same town. She was the second youngest of ten brothers and sisters.

Her father was very rich.

Sometimes we made a Sunday excursion to her childhood home, or what was left of it. Now it was tall apartment buildings and parking lots. I had to close my eyes in order to see what Mamma saw: a large white house set in a garden of fruit trees and birches. Mamma used to climb to the top of one of these trees and sit there waiting for her father to come home. On her fiftieth birthday she also climbed to the top of a tree, but that ended with a brain concussion and hospitalization.

Mamma's father died when she was ten, but they continued to live in the big house with its garden and trees until she was nineteen. She had a secure family life. The children were close to each other, and their home was always filled with people. With laughter and song and love.

Seeing pictures of Mamma when she was young makes me sad. She is lovely, her eyes are happy and full of expectation.

Why doesn't life turn out as we hope and plan?

Why is Time so merciless, stealing our opportunities if we are not swift enough to grasp them immediately?

Why is it so frightening to reach sixty because one was once sixteen and believed that time existed in infinite supply? Why couldn't one know that Time moves on with ever-increasing speed and plays havoc with all things we once thought we could leave for tomorrow?

Mamma's happiness in this picture is very like what I see in my sister's confirmation photograph. She never moved from Trondhjem, where she lives with her husband and five children. She looks a little less happy in recent photos than there where she is all dressed up holding a prayer book, embracing the whole world in her smile.

We invest so much in our dreams and hopes.

Once we were children who woke up on the morning of our confirmation day. The day we had longed for through so many years, the day when a change was to take place, when adult life was to begin, and with it the right to make our own decisions.

And in a framed photograph we line up for posterity, next

to other pictures, in which we are infants, five-year-olds, schoolchildren, brides.

We stare out into space, never to exist again.

Soon I will be an old, white-haired lady, into whose lap someone places a baby, saying: "Smile, Grandma." I who myself so recently was photographed on my grandmother's lap. I who was picking flowers just the other day cannot fathom that it may all be over tomorrow.

WE ACQUIRED OUR CAT THROUGH AN ADVERTISEMENT. THE previous owner brought it himself. Driving through half the city and out to us in the country so as to be sure it was going to a good home.

We had asked for a male, black or white.

Tasse is flecked with white and after weeks of uncertainty when we could not agree about its sex, he proved to be a she.

When young she was indescribably ugly—long and thin, with a need for love to which she gave vehement expression.

When I was writing or reading, she sat on my shoulder like a bird. Linn walked about with her on a leash and with red ribbons tied round her neck and tail. Made her dance on her hind legs or go on her forelegs like a wheelbarrow. She slept in a doll's carriage or lay patiently in a basket which the neighborhood children pulled behind them.

One day they put her in the washing machine and pressed the Start button. I cursed my laziness in not bothering to learn how the machine worked. I kept pressing knobs and turning pointers until at last the door flew open and an indignant Tasse jumped out. In my imagination I had already watched her going through the entire cycle and had decided to ask my neighbor to open the machine at the end of the spin-drying.

I plan to take her to the vet; I hear that you can get the Pill for cats. But suddenly Tasse will not let herself be caught. She keeps squirming out of my arms, her gaze becomes distant, she runs in circles in the garden, jumps in the air, and finally disappears. In the evening I am by the window watching her and realizing that Tasse, too, is feeling the spring. She is no longer thin. Her body is soft and lithe, her fur gleams, and everyone thinks she is a cat of pure ancestry.

She has four suitors and her life is love.

Every day and every night, with all of them.

Enormous tomcats with unkempt fur coats and scars and fighting wounds all over their bodies—growling and trembling, spreading a stench around our house day and night.

And Tasse wanders in and out; never lets herself be caught, as condescending to them as she is to us. Pretends she doesn't understand. Torments and teases them. And deprives us all of our night's sleep.

She'll become pregnant, all right, if she isn't so already.

Four male cats cry and suffer.

It's no use.

That's the way some are. There's nothing you can do about it.

GRANDMA STAYED WITH US AS LONG AS PAPA WAS ALIVE.
An old woman with the soul of a young girl who opened
her heart to me, because she felt we were kindred spirits.

She recreated the world, making it a wonderful place in
which everything might happen. In which a tree or a stone
was so much more than what we could see with our eyes. She
showed me how the veins in leaves were alive and pulsating.
And she was the first to tell me that plants cried out when you
hurt them.

On our walks nature was part of the kingdom of heaven,
with God keeping watch behind his curtain of cloud and sun
and stars.

Everything that grew had its beauty, a life of its own. We
never spoke of conservation; but Grandma taught me that I
had no right to dominate nature, violate it, as if I were not
responsible for the whole.

A face with heavy features and lots of wrinkles. Two eyes
in which the whites had become yellow, but in the center still
a lovely light blue. The good smell when I rested my head
against her chest. The warmth of her embrace.

It was not until I was grown up that it occurred to me that
Grandma was an old woman. I noticed that the back on which
I had hung was bowed and bent. The hair of which she had
boasted—how the boys had loved to pull it when she was a
little girl—had become a thin white pigtail that she twisted
into a little bun at the back of her head.

We lived in Trondhjem, she in Oslo, but I often stayed
with her in the summer. And when I was seventeen I went to
live in Oslo for a year. Sometimes we went to three cinema
performances in one evening. Grandma paid. We went to
small cafés and discussed the people sitting around us.

Best of all was staying the night in her room. We had to keep quiet, because Grandma's landlady had forbidden guests.

The desk by the window. Nobody had such exciting drawers as she, full of letters and boxes and jewelry and things. Memories from a long life.

Sometimes we cried over Grandfather's love letters.

They had been divorced for many years when he died. Everybody said he had left her because she was difficult and bad. This I never understood. We used to sit on her golden bedspread, eyes fixed on Grandfather's picture above the bookcase, lingering there for a long time before moving on to a photograph of Papa. Her voice when she told me about the time when she was the young wife of an officer and Papa a small boy—nicer than any other small boy in the whole world. Grandfather coming home in the evening in his splendid uniform and picking them up one after the other.

Grandma's unhappy marriage. A divorce in which she was made the scapegoat, although it was he who immediately re-married. I never asked Granny what happened; I knew that her thoughts did not now go beyond the happy years. Almost all the time I knew Grandma she lived in a world of fantasy more real to her than any unpleasant memories. And in this world the two of us would wander for hours on end.

The year when I was seventeen in Oslo and my best friend was seventy-five.

It hurts to remember the last part of her life. An old-people's home. Tastefully furnished. All the colors harmonizing, staff in white aprons and patient smiles. Yet as soon as the bell rang for breakfast, lunch or supper, the fifty old ladies immediately had to leave their rooms and troop to the dining room. Sit at table with people whose company they had not sought. Converse about events in which they had no interest.

Find friends when loneliness and waiting were the only things they had in common.

The panic if she had to spend a day in bed; three days in bed meant being transferred to the nursing-home wing. There was a long waiting list for residents' rooms, and seldom did anyone return from the nursing home. One day Grandma, too, was moved there.

"It is much better for the old one to have constant supervision, be able to stay with others in the same situation." Relatives who only want the best for their dear ones, and send them to an institution where one is no longer "I" but "we."

"We" have to go to bed a little early, perhaps—if "we" have managed to get up at all that day. Sometimes the evening wash and preparation for the night takes place at four in the afternoon. A little early, maybe, but there is a great shortage of staff—and "we" don't have all that much to do anyway when "we" are up.

Knocking on the door is no longer necessary. What sort of secrets can an old person have? One who has only her bed a scant three feet from her neighbor's. Where there are no longer books or furniture or pictures. According to the rules. But if the nurse is kind, "we" may be able to hang a photograph on the wall. (But better not use a nail—they leave a nasty mark.) Thus "we" can lie there and stare at pictures of family and friends who have so much to do in their own lives that visiting the old one is put off from week to week. After all, "we" are so comfortable. At times it can seem that visitors are a nuisance.

I remember Grandma showing me around. She opened the door of the television cabinet and wondered what had happened to the nice girl who usually was in there. I refused to believe she had become senile and wanted to call her back. Tell her that she mustn't retreat into a stupor. Remind her that I loved her and longed to share experiences as we used to do. She was not to feel that she no longer belonged to the life she had been such a rich part of.

I sat at her bedside and stole a frightened glance at her neighbor. There lay someone who had long ago entered a world where you can dream and remember in peace.

I held Grandma's hand, didn't know any longer how to talk to her. Only knew she would soon follow her neighbor into that land of dreams. Because she could not bear the situation she was in.

She had reached the moment in life where you are finally allowed to peek into the answer book. And there was no answer.

Life never became what she wished it to be. And the end was more devastating than anything else. When I went to see her, she asked who I was. It was as if we had never embraced when I was a little girl. She no longer knew that once the two of us shared the most wonderful secrets.

And so I almost stopped going to see her.

Grandma died and nothing was ever the same.

Perhaps it is foolish to attach oneself to someone who has to go so much earlier.

WHEN I WAS SEVENTEEN, I REFUSED TO GO TO SCHOOL anymore. Mamma marched me from the principal to a psychologist and to the family, but it did no good. I could no longer face sitting in a classroom with all that boredom.

I wanted to get out into the world.

One month later I was standing on the deck of a steamer, watching an English harbor materialize. It looked gray and unfamiliar. I was afraid. In the early morning I went ashore in Newcastle. A boarding school was to be my first stop. I stood it for exactly a fortnight. There were six girls in my dormitory. One of them wanted to sleep in the same bed with me. In order not to offend her, I told her I was engaged. No one was allowed to use lipstick or powder, or to wear jewelry. The headmistress stood in the doorway the first evening, steel-gray hair impeccably plaited in a circle round her head. She gazed at me severely as I lay there, the image of a homesick seventeen-year-old.

"You had your elbows on the table at dinner. This we are not accustomed to here."

Once a week we walked in a platoon into the city. Our uniform was quite becoming. If one of us wanted to buy something, we all stopped, and the rest waited while the would-be purchaser went inside with the headmistress. Window-shopping was considered vulgar, so we never did it. There was a dance on Saturday. Great excitement and laughter in the dormitories. We put our hair in paper curlers and rubbed our cheeks red. On the stroke of seven the girls from another school marched into the hall. The dance could begin. I was honored by a tango with the headmistress because I was new. She guided me with experienced hands.

On Monday morning I stood trembling in front of my

dancing partner of Saturday, telling her that unfortunately I could not stay there any longer. She looked as if she agreed. Words poured from her mouth, all disapproving.

In the train to London I felt I wanted to laugh and sing to everyone I encountered.

I took a room in the YWCA and felt that now my theatre studies would begin. Papa had left me two thousand crowns. If I was careful and had a little help from Mamma, I reckoned I should be able to manage for at least six months.

Up on the top floor I unpacked my two suitcases, made myself at home in a room for five, where the bed by the window was to be mine. Here I could lie in the morning and look at the poisonous smoke which at the end of the fifties still hung thickly over the city. I was immensely pleased with myself and life's possibilities. Standing on my own feet for the first time—and no Mamma to watch every step they took.

In the bed next to mine was an Englishwoman. She had married a Norwegian, who ran away to England, leaving her in a small Norwegian town without a penny. Now she was in London to look for him. She had borrowed money for the journey, and her face was gray and tired when she showed me photographs of her daughter. Sometimes, when she thought the rest of us were asleep, I heard her crying with the eiderdown over her head. Or she would lock herself in the bathroom, which was the only place one could be alone. Looking at the closed door, hearing her sigh despairingly in there, I wished that love would always be light and uncomplicated for me.

Every morning I worked with Irene Brent. She was both actress and teacher. My instruction was free, partly because she was a passionate friend of Norway, but also because I was a grateful audience for her recitations. She tried out all her radio and stage programs on me. Once I was even allowed to appear with her and read Norwegian poetry.

Twice a month she held open house. The strangest people of all ages—but with a common bond of burning interest in the theatre—filled her little apartment. We read aloud to each other, allotted parts, sat huddled on the few seats or on the floor. There were never any refreshments, but nobody seemed to miss them as we sat, heads bowed over tattered books of poems or plays.

Sometimes a handsome older man, who once had played Hamlet on the real stage, would visit. He was in poor health and very modest. When he appeared everyone made an extra fuss over him. Let him choose the part he wanted—or read poetry if he felt more like it. They whispered to me that life had been difficult for him, and I felt I was in the presence of a genius.

After some weeks I was allowed to accompany Irene to the school where she taught. The most famous pupil they had had there was Stewart Granger. Pictures of him were in every room. In my imagination I saw mine hanging there, too, in a few years' time.

When I didn't have anything else to do (and most of the time I had nothing else to do) I went to the cinema. Three, four performances a day.

Little coffee shops serving lovely hot chocolate. The best and cheapest lunch in the world. Sometimes I was spoken to by a stranger and could either purse my lips and act the virtuous girl from Trondhjem or experience ten exciting minutes of glances and talk, after which my courage deserted me and my "fiancé at home" entered the conversation.

I walked Bond Street and window-shopped for dresses that looked more elegant than the ones in Norway. I stared at all the lights and the crowds in Piccadilly Circus. Gaped at the

English girls, who didn't wear woolen stockings or underpants in the winter and almost all of whom seemed to have blue legs in the summer. This was the year a lonely little man was revealed as being a mass murderer who kept the bodies of women sealed in a room just across the street from my favorite cinema. Wild stories of white-slave traffic circulated among the girls at the YWCA, and some were taken home by anxious parents.

We who came from Norway saw television for the first time. Cried with Grace Kelly at her wedding and dreamed of our own. We ate Norwegian food and longed to be back home. Made expensive collect calls to ask if the family could send a little more money.

Some of the girls left the YWCA because they weren't allowed to be out after ten o'clock without special permission. Others took jobs as domestic help or met an Englishman and married him. But most, like me, became a bit better at English and went back home to Norway again.

Linn wants to become a tightrope dancer in the circus. She writes long letters to Ringling Brothers. What is bothering her is whether she will have to live with the circus while she is learning the craft.

I see no sorrow in her eyes at the thought she will have to part from me. It is the luggage that worries her: what clothes and books to bring. In her faraway look, so unaffected by leaving Mamma, I can see a time to come . . . perhaps in only a few years. And I am grateful, because I see a glimpse of what I one day will go through.

A parting where I am the one who weeps. While her mind has long been on a path where I can never follow her.

WE ARE ON A BICYCLE TRIP.

A mother who has to lose weight and a seven-year-old daughter who has just received her first two-wheeler from her father. It is blue and shiny, and gleams and sparkles with an air of superiority next to my old and worn machine, which is older than my child. One bell goes pling in a slightly rusty voice and a fragile one responds.

The adult breast is filled with love and tenderness as a thin little figure that has just arrogantly sped by half turns to look back. A dirty hand gives a quick, eager wave. A smile that can't quite disguise the solemn pride.

It is spring, she has a bicycle from her father, and Mamma has time today.

We are almost like an ordinary family.

Now and again we ride side by side. We talk to the trees we pass, about how hot the sun is, although it is only spring, about the wild flowers we are going to take home and put in vases on the kitchen table.

And when we get tired of talking, we pretend that my big bicycle is chatting with her little one. They have so much to discuss. My bicycle tells what the world was like before the little girl was born. It lived, then, in the center of Oslo, and it was always afraid. There was so much traffic and the girl's mother didn't know the regulations. So that when they were out together they were always followed by blaring horns and angry shouts.

Later it moved to an island in Sweden and there there were almost no cars. Mamma preferred bicycling along the paths through the woods, which were so narrow the trees sometimes made nasty scratches on the paint.

Now, in its old age, it is good to live in the country and feel useful, because none of the baby-sitters or friends or family are ever afraid of asking to borrow it.

And that's nice. Not to stay in a cellar and rust.

"And what about you, little bike?"
A squeaky voice explains that it is her first spring and she is a little afraid of falling and scratching her paint.

My bicycle tells the other about the coming winter and how lonely it can be standing in the dark among the garden furniture and wheelbarrows and spades, never knowing when the cellar door will open to announce, through new activity, that spring is coming. In the winter she prefers just to stand and pretend to be asleep; after all, you can't have a decent conversation with a wheelbarrow.

Sometimes she has to close her ears to the hammock, which is only a year old and is large, blue and important, speaks disparagingly to her because her colors are faded and she no longer has a baggage rack.

"Oh, Mamma," Linn says, "can't we buy a baggage rack and tool bag?"
Quickly I have to let my bike explain that she is too old to carry so much extra ballast.

We talk to the trees we pass. Call encouragement to them because they look so large and heavy and rather naked since the leaves haven't yet sprouted.

"Is it dangerous to stay out at night?" Linn calls to them.

"Oh, no," a tree answers in a growly voice. "We have each other's company. It must be worse to be a bicycle propped against a garden fence, when it's dark and Linn is in bed asleep and no longer able to look after it."

"Mamma, do you think the bicycles are afraid?"

The big bicycle answers that perhaps it is a bit scary on a dark, windy night. Sometimes, then, it can be very lonely.

"Oh, Mamma," Linn sighs.

And then we are back home.

The child doesn't want to go in.

She sits on the steps patting the old, ugly bicycle. Her eyes are moist and I have to sit down beside her and remind her that we were just playing, that it was make-believe.

We sit there a long time and get chilly bottoms.

Finally, the big bicycle has to say that now she would like to be left in peace. She can think so much better when she is alone. Besides, she isn't really afraid or lonely in the night. That was only something she had said to make herself interesting. Trees are always very friendly company, and the firs around the house often talk to her.

During supper Linn keeps running to the window—looks at the trees and the big and the little bicycle. But we don't talk about them anymore because there is a children's television program, some reading out loud, and evening prayers.

When I tuck her in and she has gone to sleep, I can hear her sigh as if she were having sad dreams.

Before I go to bed, an old and a new bicycle roll into the vestibule, to light and warmth, outer garments, and the pretty green table inlaid with brown stones.

That's where they now stand every night. After all, one can never be completely sure. . . .

THE NORWEGIAN THEATRE IS ON TOUR WITH *A Doll's House.*

Spring is early this year, warm and pleasant. It is welcomed with flimsy blouses as if spring were summer.

We drive through Hardanger. It is so beautiful that it hurts inside. I didn't know that my country was also this. Mountains reflected in placid, glittering fjords—mountains reaching up to a sky filled with sun. Here and there, snow on a shady slope.

The road is a journey through several seasons.

What will become fruits are now beautiful flowers. Soft, delicate colors which multiply across the hill, where wild flowers I have never seen before flock in blue and red and yellow, and we *see* the fragrance before we open the windows and let the apple and cherry blossoms pour into the bus and intoxicate us all.

For a while we are high up, surrounded by snow-capped mountains which have never heard of the spring we just passed through.

Narrow, winding roads—at times we have to put the heavy bus in reverse and let the hind wheels hang almost beyond the road in order to be able to proceed.

Cataracts in wild plunges down the mountainsides, as if they are beside themselves with joy because their coat of ice has disappeared. Changing in the light—billions of diamonds on their way to the sea.

"Oh, this Norway, I understand how one can suffer a little for it."

We have our own orchestra and can celebrate all this beauty. A fiddler sits next to me, thin and bony, with a violin under his chin. And now I *experience* the "Bridal Procession in Hardanger," and know why the Hardanger fiddle best expresses Norwegian nature.

Happy is the one who can spend a day in California, drink the juice from an orange that has just been picked from the tree, feel the heat as a caress over body and face—and then the next day walk on board a little ferry and stand in its bow and glide into a Norwegian fjord and know that one is part of all this.

In our tour bus there are three of us who all auditioned for the theatre school the same year. None of us made it. Now we meet in the evening onstage, in leading roles. Our failures lie far back in time, and much has happened since. We sit in the bus and reminisce.

"How did you react to it?"

"Can you remember who was admitted that year?"

"What did you do afterward? That night? The following months?"

We laugh. Feel happy together about something that once hurt so very much.

I WAS SOON TO BE EIGHTEEN AND HAD ARRIVED IN OSLO after studying acting in London. I was convinced that I knew almost everything. There was never any doubt about my own potential as an actress.

Yet deep inside me there was a feeling of uncertainty and a longing for the school in Trondhjem, where friends were now studying for university entrance exams, living in a security of school and studies and home and friends.

I was going to stay all by myself for the first time in my life. I had a one-room apartment with its own entrance, and I thought I was going to begin at the theatre school.

After my audition—Juliet and Ophelia—I stood in a corridor and waited for the list to be posted of those who had been accepted. And when it happened, a tall, awkward boy placed himself next to me and read aloud the names of the chosen ones. While something was dying within me, because *I* was not included, I understood, when he suddenly stopped at the next-to-the-last name, that he was. He barely smiled, and walked quietly out of the room as if nothing had happened to him.

For years I followed his career. I hoped to find some justice in my defeat by seeing his success.

Now he is a fish dealer in Sweden and, I hear, very satisfied with things.

I stood in the corridor a long time until at last I knew all ten names by heart. Some of the older students walked past and nodded to me. And then I walked out into the street. I walked all night, shocked and with a foreboding that this was the way my life would always be. Like the balls at the dancing school, where the successful ones were separated from the others. Where the loser in a pink dress stood crying in the ladies' room.

It never occurred to me that there must have been a number of losers that day. Future colleagues whom I would meet a long time later in a tour bus. That we would lightly trade back and forth the young people we once were, with laughter and distance.

Then I only had Grandma. By morning I was with her, and I cried my heart out. Sobbed on a breast which never had harbored the dream that now was crushed within me. In the span of a night everything that was customary and familiar had been stripped away, and I was in the middle of a transition. There was something to be learned from this, something hard to understand: that one carries one's fate within oneself, one's fate is not dependent on this kind of failure or success.

To become conscious is a long process, to become open to sorrow, look upon it as part of living, of developing, of changing.

A year in Oslo, where the first few months of loneliness are what I remember best. Where not being able enough, talented enough, was the big sorrow. Months that seemed endless, without any goal or meaning. Carefully jotted down in a blue diary that I still have, written by a young girl who lived long ago. Pains that I no longer recall, joys that are no longer a part of me.

An apartment twelve feet square. Days without structure. Long nights filled with bad dreams. An eternity between getting up in the morning and the forsaken feeling at night.

I had the library as a fixed point every day. Hours spent with accurate notes on what I read. Large, silent rooms. A place to be, a place to belong.

There were students and retired people and housewives. In the winter there were the homeless, who were freezing and would sit with a newspaper until closing time, when the hunt for a night's shelter once again resumed.

No one spoke to anyone else—no contact with the neighbor. One would turn pages gently, not to disturb or attract attention.

Once I had tea in a café across the street. A girl, a bit older than I, sat down at my table. We talked for an hour. That is, she talked and didn't seem to notice that I was shy and just a grateful listener. For weeks I returned to the same table, fantasized about all the things we could do together. But she never came back.

Occasionally I would get work—licking stamps, addressing envelopes, whatever was available. At such times I had dinner every day and wrote home that my acting career was progressing nicely.

THE TOUR BUS IS A BLESSING. HERE THERE ARE NO DE-
mands. I am thinking of what Victor Borge once said: that he
loved to be onstage because there no telephone could reach
him.

I have hours of pleasant chatting with my neighbor. Experience nature in my own country. At times some of us will
start out early in the morning on foot, and are flushed and
happy when the bus overtakes us.

There is the anticipation of coming to a new place every
day, meeting a new audience each evening. Communicating
with people who are not accustomed to the theatre. Acting for
men and women who still consider it worthwhile bicycling or
walking long distances to see a play. An audience packed into
a little hall with uncomfortable benches. An aged stage and
poor lighting.

We are the theatre group. We have eaten at a strange
hotel, phoned home to children and spouses, made up at tem-
porary dressing tables.

They are the public, who live their own lives down there in
the darkness. Their breathing and their laughter and their
stirrings are part of our experience of them. Now and then a
chord is struck, we are one. The auditorium is still and the
stage alive.

Back at the hotel, there is wine and candlelight into the
early morning for some of us. The next day we are off again to
another place. A bus laden with costumes and scenery and
suitcases. And a few people who for a brief period live together.

One morning I have a lump in my stomach. The sort of
lump you get when you are sad for no particular reason. The
person next to me has the same feeling. We wonder what

such a sudden sorrow is caused by. And then it disappears when we share it.

We travel to small rural communities that larger companies bypass. We play to packed houses. Sometimes they have to send out for extra chairs from neighboring houses.

Seljord boasts a statue of my great-grandfather. It stands by the road and I am proud as we drive past. He started a new school here, one of the first of its kind in Norway. He is better known in this part of the country than I am.

I once met his nephew in Oslo.

I was young and newly married and working at the theatre where I am now. He was a short, thin bachelor of seventy-five, a government archivist, and like me, someone the family preferred to overlook.

One evening he was standing at the stage door and informing me he was my great-uncle. Would I honor him by dining with him the following week? Naturally, my husband was welcome as well. We arranged to meet at the Valkyrie restaurant.

I didn't even bother to dress up. I persuaded my husband to come with me so that we could laugh about it together afterward.

We were ceremoniously received by the headwaiter. Suddenly there was elegance in the old restaurant. Earlier I used to associate it with beer-drinking and meatballs. Our coats were carefully removed. The cloakroom attendant whispered that Mr. Ullmann waited for us upstairs. There was respect in his voice. Great-uncle was "known" and certainly no dunce whom two young people could believe they were coming to see as an act of charity.

The table was decorated with flowers. I was presented with a rose and my husband a carnation for his buttonhole.

The old man was wearing a worn black suit. His hair, what he had left, was combed and plastered to his head. He was nervous and his hands were cold when he welcomed us.

It was to be one of the most beautiful evenings I have ever had.

The menu and the conversation were carefully prepared, and once I stopped feeling ashamed of having turned up in jeans, prepared to be amused by the whole thing, I came closer to Papa's family than I had ever been before.

With each course there was a little speech. Enthusiastic words about what the family stood for. By the time we reached dessert, the three of us sat there, much moved, and raised our glasses to each other.

I asked questions and he spoke. Gave me a genealogy he had meticulously drawn in a flowery old man's writing.

Then just as solemnly as we had been received, it was indicated that the dinner was over.

Great-uncle had enjoyed himself enormously, but he was an old man and now he needed to rest.

His thin hand almost disappeared in mine. I gave him a quick hug. He cleared his throat and looked embarrassed.

I sent him flowers two or three times, and a letter, but had so much to do that I postponed asking him home.

Once I saw him walking along the pavement toward me. But not knowing what to say, I quickly crossed the street. Then I ran back after him to tell him how fond I was of him. I was also afraid he might have seen me. But I couldn't find him. Shortly afterward I read in the paper that he had died. I did not go to the funeral. That day I did not want to meet the rest of the family.

LINN'S VOICE ON THE TELEPHONE. THERE IS DISTANCE AND reserve. I assure her of my love. "Little one, I care more for you than anyone else."

"No, you don't."

The child's voice cuts deep.

I am still in the tour bus jolting along toward another out-of-the-way part of Norway. Almost always on the way somewhere. Seldom home. And I see the nurses and neighbors holding my daughter, doing what my arms and my hands should be doing. Perhaps she is aware of their pity, which I am sure they do feel, even though they try to hide it from her.

I realize that to them my profession and my success amount to failure, because I am not filling my place in the home where they are substituting for me. The critical thoughts which I guess they have—I understand them, because they are also mine.

I am sitting in a bus surrounded by people, and I am afraid that my loneliness will also become my daughter's. For me, loneliness functions. But maybe she longs for any kind of relationship to make up for what I have not given her.

I remember my own childhood, when one was alone in one's world and watched the big grownups and wondered at all their activity. Everything they did seemed so important just because one did not understand it and because they always looked busy. One was small and on the outside of it all, because there didn't seem to be room for children in that world of grownups.

Linn shall have something really nice when I come home. I shall take her to the theatre and the movies. Have her on my lap and tell her about when Mamma was a little girl. All this I will do when the tour is finished. Before the telephone begins to ring, before the demands from all the people who own my life become more insistent than hers.

We shall have days of belonging together; but gradually my conscience will start limiting me—the letters unanswered, the things undone. And gradually I will become the professional woman again, and be onstage or in front of a camera or at meetings, and think of her there at home, whom I always seem to fail because I can't find any solution through which her childhood and my life as an adult woman can be combined.

As people do in books, and as I think other women manage to do in *their* homes.

"THERE'S A YOUNG GIRL IN ME WHO REFUSES TO DIE. . . ."

The theatre school did not want her. But a little provincial theatre needed someone her age.

The great day came. A train left the Oslo station on its way to Stavanger. She was eighteen, sparkling with happiness—now at last it was going to happen! Securely tucked away in her handbag was a stage contract, already grubby from being continually admired, from fingers that opened and refolded it again and again. Shown to everyone who asked to see it—also to many who didn't.

The salary was six hundred dollars a year, the happiness worth millions. The first part she was given was that of Anne Frank. Like thousands of young girls all over the world, she was to live Anne's thoughts and Anne's fate. Hope with her. Believe with her.

Like most who interpreted Anne Frank, she was an immediate success. In the radiant innocence of that little Jewish girl she recognized something of herself, her own dream that love was the most important thing—and would outlive a world that appeared pointless.

Roses and letters, interviews and sudden fame. Without too much effort she was someone they had to reckon with. She belonged to the theatre, could call herself an actress, even though officially she was still a pupil.

This was how she had hoped it would be. If she could only get on the stage, her ability would no longer languish in shadows and dreams. She thirsted for compliments as a confirmation that earlier fiascos no longer had meaning. People must love her, and if she was responsive and clever enough, she would be able to retain that love after the curtain had gone down. She had a burning desire that the public's love for her should endure even after she had washed off the make-up. Worth was measured by the number of people who admired her as a woman, by the extent to which she lived up to others' expectations. The façade must be free of scratches. She became anxious to please. She forgot that she had been alone, unsure. She forgot that there was another world beyond the stage.

When I made my debut as Anne Frank the critics wrote that I *was* Anne. I don't believe this meant that my life or my stage interpretation or appearance had direct parallels with the heroine of the diary, but that I really borrowed Anne's soul for those two hours on the stage. Let Anne play Anne. Many years passed before I again experienced such complete identification.

My acting was not pretense, but reality.

I knew that it was theatre, but it was a reality that belonged to the theatre. It was like when I was a child. I lived in fantasy, yet I employed real emotions and longings within those fantasies. Now I became indignant if anyone suggested that it was only a role.

"I'm not acting, I'm not deceiving."

Within those walls in Stavanger I thought I had found what I was seeking.

I would arrive early in the morning, feeling at home in this half-darkness; the dusty air, the cramped dressing rooms, the stage with its worn slanted boards—the place in the world where I most wanted to be. Rehearsals and discussions without anyone watching the clock. The buzz in the auditorium before the curtain went up. The arc lights. The excitement. The audience. The tension. The part that was to live its own life. Weep with a role. Laughter and yearning and fury borrowed from an imaginary person. Emotions I had scarcely known. The eyes and expressions and movements of my colleagues. Sometimes we were so close it seemed unreal there existed other relationships outside the theatre. Surely no love, no hatred, could be stronger than the passions that quivered on the stage between eight and half-past ten each evening.

For most, this complete absorption by one's profession belongs only to the first years.

But some very few never find their way back to life outside the stage. They grow old, and they take your hand, and they recite a speech they spoke in 1930. Hamlet or King Lear sits in front of you and you feel slightly embarrassed because you are afraid some thoughtless remark might wake somebody from a lovely dream which has lasted a whole professional life.

And even longer.

I REMEMBER TOURS ON WHICH EVERYBODY DID EVERY-
thing. Little boardinghouses with poor food. The sour land-
ladies who looked suspiciously at our suitcases when we left.
Or the fourposter in a little country vicarage where I was put
up for the night and where the clergyman himself brought
coffee and homemade rolls for breakfast.

The rented-room life. An elderly couple who treated me
like a daughter. Saw that I drank a glass of milk in the morning, scolded me gently if I came home late or left my little
attic room too untidy. Kindness I can never return.

I would have dinner at Guri's. Her apartment was open to
those who lived in rented rooms, mostly men. She was big and
fat and full of energy; her hair was gray and short-cropped.
Her face had never seen a trace of make-up. I don't know how
old she was.

She was mercilessly critical before you passed through the
eye of her needle and became a regular guest. She exposed
any affectation or pretentiousness instantly. Everyone called
her Guri, as if she had been born and was going to die without a surname. She was an institution in the town where she
lived. She came from Jaeren, a wind-blown, stony part of the
country which seemed to have fashioned in her a picture of
itself.

Sometimes romance blossomed at Guri's dining table. But
not very often; her eagle eye was always on the watch and no
woman bore off one of Guri's favorites without a fight. Con-
firmed spinster that she was, she preferred to see her home as
a place for singing, folk dancing, cards and lavish meals than
as a place for evenings of flirtation. She snorted at loving
couples, but turned up dutifully at the weddings, all over
Norway, for which she was partly responsible.

She sat in her large brown chair, which no one else would have dreamed of taking, the inevitable cigarette between thumb and middle finger of one hand—while the index finger of her other hand directed every conversation or song. And we often sang.

Friendships were made for life. Young people matured there. And many older people found a milieu they had lacked in their youth. We were a motley group. A strange mixture of professions and talents and wisdom and diffidence. With an old woman binding us together. As if she had always existed in this half-lit apartment surrounded by her court.

We all loved her and were a little afraid of her. We all fought for her favor. She stamped her black-wool-stockinged feet angrily and demonstratively if a new woman found her way to the table in tailor-made clothes and coiffed hair.

There, at Guri's, I met a young doctor. Over the coffee he indulged in fantasies about how wonderful it would be if all the women in the world would unite. Only they could save mankind. He would ride in front on a white horse leading them.

We fell in love and dreamed of the things we could do together in life. Guri came all the way to Trondhjem and brought loud laughter and friendliness to our wedding table. But she predicted that it would never last.

DINNER FOR FOUR HUNDRED GUESTS IN CANNES. WE EAT lobsters and drink champagne. Hands loaded with diamonds and pearls bring lobster claws to mouths. Celebrities at every table. And each table represents a fortune in money and apathy.

I am there too.

The person next to me talks eagerly, unconcerned that I don't understand a word. Twice I tell him that the little French I learned at school has long since flown out of my head. But he continues indefatigably. Sometimes I smile coldly at him and nod my head, now and then I turn aside a little and drink a toast with a handsome man at the next table. He keeps looking at me through half-closed eyes, and isn't eating his lobster claws.

Outside is the soft French night. I know how it feels to walk into it. From the noise in the brilliantly lit dining room—and then out into the stillness and the warmth and the sound of the sea.

I remember other dinners, all too many; if I hadn't been a guest of honor sitting next to the president of the film festival, I would have got up and slipped out and away.

White, made-up faces and then all the bronzed ones. People with time and money to follow summer all the year. Hands covered with rings (no doubt they can show tenderness and caress a loved one to sleep) nervously fluttering over the food, the wineglasses—grotesque instruments for displaying jewelry and boredom. From the next table a champagne glass is raised to me. His eyelids have almost closed. He admires himself in his spoon.

The lights are turned down. Outside, rockets are being fired and it is unbelievably beautiful.

And we get up from the table and say goodbye to each other.

I escape from the unknown admirer, who is approaching me rather unsteadily, but first I send him a passionate look, so that he will understand how much I will suffer by this painful and sudden departure. To my hotel by limousine, still being spoken to in French, and then at last alone in my room.

I sit by the window and look down at the beach below. Smile and think of another evening spent with one I loved under a spruce tree because we had nowhere else to go. Our clothes were covered with moss and grass and we laughed and were happy and alone in the world.

WE HAD BROAD GOLD RINGS. BOTH WERE SHY WHEN WE stood in the shop choosing them. We told the woman who served us that they were for someone else. I noticed that he flirted with her.

He painted eggs and hid them one evening. I had forgotten it was Easter.

Once I told him that I thought I was pregnant, but didn't want a baby. He cried.

We had a car named Charley. It was blue and not exactly new when we bought it. In the summer Charley and he and I went camping. In the evenings we wrote letters to each other saying how happy we were to be married to each other. Mornings we woke early because it was hot, with many insects in the tent.

We moved to Oslo. Neither of us was earning much. Every month we made a budget, which we kept for about three days. Later we quarreled over it.

Occasionally we visited friends or went to the cinema or the theatre. I was very fond of his family.

He specialized in psychiatry and I had my job with the Norwegian Theatre.

It was like living in a cocoon of security. Our sense of mutual closeness was that between brother and sister, where both had the same secure background. We felt satisfied with existence, lived according to accepted rules and seldom did anything out of the ordinary.

Now and again we had a bottle of red wine and laid ambitious plans for the future. I was his child and never protested when he treated me like one. He would not speak to me for a whole day after I said I wanted to take a driving test. He was sure this was a responsibility I was not fit to bear.

I was dependent, and happy that he was the stronger and wished to look after me.

Sometimes we could feel a sudden hatred of the other, because one had run into a limitation that could not be defined. We believed in a future together, yet our dreams were different.

Our marriage lasted five years.

I can never be so young again with anyone else.

THE MAN I WAS MARRIED TO ALL THOSE YEARS AGO WAS called Jappe.

I am at his fortieth birthday party. I am not the hostess. I have been placed almost at the foot of the table. But from there I can better see the man I had lived with when I was very young. He is not as slim as he had been; he looks happier, but also more tired.

His wife is everything that I was not. Part of it, perhaps, I could have become, if we had really tried.

He has a good life, I believe.

Half of the people around the table are friends we had together; and those I don't know are the ones he and she have met after my time. His brothers are there—all three of them —and their wives and his mother Astrid, and his aunt Ella, who still knits Christmas presents not only for my child, but for my sister's five as well.

There is much I remember and recognize, many threads at the table, in some of which I willingly entangle myself. But here are also deep chasms of strangeness.

I look at Jappe and feel how fond I am of him and how good it is to know that he exists.

One day he comes with his little daughter to my summer cottage. She is two years old. They stroll together over the rocks and I stand by the window and look at them. No one sees me and I cry. He is holding her hand, pointing and explaining. Oh, so patiently. And she is small and safe with him. His smile is one I have never seen.

Many years ago when we had decided to be divorced, we sat holding hands in the marriage counselor's office. He asked why we wished to separate, if we were such good friends.

"Just for that reason," we replied cheerily.

We stood in the street and said goodbye, because I was going to Ingmar in Sweden. And when we had no more cheerful words to say, we had nothing. At least nothing that ventured out.

"Bye, then," he said, and walked away. He never turned around. I turned all the time, just in case. . . . It was so strange to see him walk among all the other people. None of whom paid any attention to him. Only I knew who he was and what had happened to him.

If I could have run after him, I would have done it. But my mouth could not speak; my feet could not walk in that direction.

I was in the hospital to have Linn. I had come home to Norway, because I felt my child should be born here. Suddenly, he was standing there in his white doctor's uniform, and as he came in much of my fear left me. He sat so quietly by my bed. Now and again he took my hand and smiled. We did not speak. But he became an important part of my life that day. And I learned something about love I had not known before.

As I learned something the day, radiantly happy because of all that Ingmar and I were sharing, I went to the lawyer's office to sign the divorce papers that would make final several years' separation. Jappe had already been there. Suddenly I laid my head on the papers and sobbed. Felt I was signing Jappe out of my life.

While we were still married, I once spent a night in his room at the hospital. He was on duty and I wanted to be with him, because I am afraid to be alone at night and had an ear infection.

In the early morning a nurse rushed in and asked him to

hurry to a delivery that might become complicated. It was the first birth for which he would have sole responsibility.

I was left lying there with my inflamed ear. The eardrum burst and it was terribly painful.

When he returned, I didn't dare say anything. I lay quiet, expecting him to ask or to speak; but he, too, was silent, preoccupied with his own experience. Silence between us perhaps because it was now daybreak and each was afraid to worry the other. Afraid of losing love if we interrupted the other's thoughts. Inept in the art of giving love, our silence erased a birth and a burst eardrum.

He was a human being with whom I lived for a long time, yet it was as if we never had time to get to know one another.

More than anything I grieve over what we never said.

ONE EVENING TASSE WILL NOT STAY OUTSIDE. SUMMER HAS come, and we think the cat can sleep perfectly well in one of her two boxes on the veranda. She claws at the window, meows and looks beseechingly at me where I sit reading. But I am hard-hearted.

When I have gone to bed and turned off the light, I hear her sad wailing again. Somehow she has found her way to my bedroom window and placed herself beneath it, trying to persuade me. Our Tasse, who has made love to four unkempt wild cats. Now she sounds like a princess. When I come to the window she no longer meows with sound. Only the mouth opens in a silent imploring prayer. I note the effect for future use on the stage.

Severely I tell Tasse to go away. Advise her there is no hope of her being allowed in.

I return to bed, listen to her voice in the night, and then at last it is quiet. I sleep. Half an hour later, suddenly there are two of them. Two voices longingly and beseechingly intertwined. Two cats' voices just under my window.

It is the first time since Tasse's wild night with the neighborhood gang that I see her with one of them. He is the best-looking, a black-and-white one. The one I had hoped would become the father of her inevitable kittens.

Now they are sitting there side by side, meowing up at me, as if together asking for Tasse's immediate admittance to the house.

During the cat concerto out there in the summer night I fall asleep and don't wake again until Linn comes running in in the morning, saying that Tasse is waiting on the veranda with a kitten in her mouth.

We run out. She gives me a melancholy look. As if my lack

of understanding has been the cause of all her suffering. Beside her crawls a blind miniature of the black-and-white companion of last night. Just like Tasse to give birth to only one.

We fetch Linn's old cradle and arrange a beautiful bed on the veranda. Some difference of opinion with the new mother, who insists on taking her baby into my closet.

In the end, she settles down outside in the sunlight and fragrance of flowers, shaded by parasols and tables. She is treated like a queen.

In the course of that day I see a mother being born.

Not all at once. In the beginning she leaps up every time someone walks past. Runs after them to see if anything interesting is happening. The kitten has to tag along, hanging from her breast as if it were no part of her, a foreign thing that had suddenly attached itself to her body.

She continually wants to get inside the house; we have to carry her back to the kitchen, which she tries to evade. We have to admonish her. She looks at her newly born with resignation and absent-mindedly washes it.

But when the sun paints the sky red in the afternoon—Tasse has become a mother. She lies in her basket, serene and relaxed. Looks condescendingly at us when we peer down at her baby. One paw protectively over it. Indifferently she watches the festive fare we bring and only deigns to eat when no one is looking. Mundane thoughts one must not suspect in this supermother.

Linn sits patiently beside her and reminds her discreetly of their old games. But the days have gone once and for all when Tasse would walk around with red ribbons on her tail.

A Doll's House IS ON TOUR AGAIN. THIS TIME WE ARE competing with the midnight sun in northern Norway. For a week I am unable to sleep because it is so beautiful there.

What a country I live in! Snow-capped mountains and the smell of heather and bog. A fresh breath of air from water that is pure, from fjords that wind into the strangest hidden places. Where in summer the sun never disappears, just kisses the horizon before it rises again and sets off on its journey across the sky.

People who spontaneously show what they are feeling, and talk in eager singing voices, as if they cannot get over their delight at being out of the eternal darkness of winter.

North Norway when the thermometer records ninety degrees and I lie naked on the bed without a quilt and the light beats on the windowpanes all night.

I have traveled all over the world, and I'm quite certain that for me no impressions have been stronger than those I experience now. The contrasts here are so immense. The sea so bottomless when I lean over a ship's rail and imagine all the adventure deep down in the water. The mountains towering over me on all sides, wild and barren, closer to heaven than I thought mountains could get.

To feel the wind and the sun on the face—and at the same time feel the fragrance of trees and rocks and the earth I walk on touch the skin—that is part of what changes my life.

WHEN I WAS TWENTY-TWO, PETER PALITZSCH, A GERMAN director, came to our theatre in Oslo. He had been Bertolt Brecht's closest collaborator and for many years one of the leading directors with the Berliner Ensemble in East Berlin. When the Wall was built he was in Norway staging *The Caucasian Chalk Circle* and he elected not to go back. In the East his friends and colleagues put an advertisement in a paper: "We had a friend; he exists no more." They went to his apartment and burned all his private letters and pictures.

We who knew him in those days looked at him secretly and wondered how he could bear it. He never spoke about it. His only possessions were the contents of two suitcases and a few picture postcards pinned on the wall of his hotel room.

He taught me that everything we portray on the stage ought to be shown from two sides. Be illustrated in both black and white. When I smile, I must also show the grimace behind it. Try to depict the countermovement—the counter-emotion.

I learned to work more consciously.

I remember the opening scene of *The Chalk Circle*. At the first reading I thought I was to play a woman in a heroic situation. Her name was Grusha.

Revolution had come to the village where she lived in poverty. Everyone had fled the murder and fire that followed in the wake of war. While she herself was running away she found an infant abandoned by its mother. She stopped without knowing what she would do with the little bundle wrapped in silk and velvet, precious materials that she had never touched before.

My interpretation was to sit down and look tenderly and

softly at the baby. Sing to it, pick it up, and then take it with me.

"Think a bit deeper," the director said. "Show her doubts, surely she must have had some? Her cowardice: don't you feel it? And what about her ambivalence in the face of this new responsibility? The audience will sympathize with you anyway. Even if they don't grasp everything you are trying to illustrate, they will recognize you as acting in a way they themselves might have acted. No spontaneous nobility. Not necessarily symbolizing goodness all the time."

My interpretation became this:

The woman is sitting with the baby, but puts it down as she realizes what a hindrance it will be on her flight. She stands up and walks away. Stops. Doubt. Turns back. Reluctantly sits down again. Looks at the little bundle. Looks away. Then, finally, she picks it up with a gesture of resignation and runs on. Without joy and without any great emotions, she starts a new life with the child. Rebukes it for the difficulties it has caused her. Laughs at its pitifulness and helplessness. Her maternal feelings are not immediately aroused; are not given any romantic expression.

Only then, when no situation or character is obviously good or evil, is it truly interesting to act.

Like all great directors, Peter Palitzsch never told me what I should think or do every moment of the time. He worked on the actor's imagination and musicality. It is only the untalented director who imagines himself in every part, wants his own thoughts and emotions portrayed; it is only the untalented who makes his own limitations those of the actor as well.

Peter worked with the Norwegian company as if he were a conductor. He brought us together like an orchestra; our different temperaments were the instruments.

I, who for years had kept Stanislavski's book on the art of acting on my bedside table, now began to look for other ways.

Partly, I found a new technique which seemed right for me. I placed more weight on details, something that would benefit me later in films, where close-ups allow subtlety to emerge more distinctly than on the stage.

Less feelings, more concentration on giving expression to the feelings.

In one of his books Ingmar Bergman describes a scene from *Persona* in which Bibi Andersson has a long erotic monologue and I am listening to it: "If you look at Liv's face, you'll see that all the time it's swelling. It's fascinating—her lips get bigger, her eyes darker, the whole girl is transformed into a sort of greed. There is a profile shot of Liv, here, which is incomparable. One can see her face transformed into a sort of cold, voluptuous mask. . . . When we were going to shoot it, I told Liv that she must gather all her feeling into her lips. She had to concentrate on placing her sensibility there—it's possible, you know, to place your feeling in different parts of the body. Suddenly you can summon your emotions into your little finger, or your big toe, or your buttock, or your lips. And that is what I insisted she did." Technique.

But there also has to be an inner balance between technique and intuition. Intuition had been my strong point as an actress. Now Peter Palitzsch taught me to place it in context. He never interfered with my expression, but was always testing my motivation. He taught me to observe myself, to let the part play itself with the help of what I knew about the character I was portraying.

Grusha is sitting beside the baby whose mother has abandoned it, and as she bends down to pick it up, a tear comes into her eye and rolls down her cheek. Suddenly the tear is there and it is a wonderful feeling. What I tried to do was to be open. So what happened to Grusha would happen through me. I was open to her tears and her emotions.

Then it is fantastic when the tears come, and I am surprised because I hadn't known she would weep at that moment. But it is no longer myself caught in an emotion, not *I* that weep.

I HANG UP THE TELEPHONE AND I FEEL SAD. LINN STUDIES me and asks if it was a stupid conversation. I nod and feel a sudden wild desire to confide.

And that is what I do.

"You should go for a think-walk," Linn suggests.

"A think-walk?"

The child explains that sometimes she puts on pretty clothes, a nightgown of mine, a bow from an old teddy bear, an umbrella or a balloon in her hand, and goes out. Looks at the flowers and the trees and stops to chat with the people she meets.

"Then you forget why you are sad. Do it, Mamma—go for a think-walk."

And that is what I do.

It is summer of the year I have spent at home in Oslo.

I am sitting on a bench outside my house eating homemade waffles with jam, forgetting that I want to lose weight. The heat is buzzing in my head.

In Los Angeles no one would understand what it is like to have a feast of waffles in the sun after a long, dark winter. Life there is so remote from this.

I wonder if I experience it as real. I can see the falseness, the frivolity, clearly enough, but no one forces me to take it seriously. Although I am easily seduced. It is like a play in the theatre, where one takes the sets and the lighting and the costumes as a means of expressing what is real. There is always content beyond. Like in life. When it has its basis in a form. When it has its basis in me. When I am exercising my profession.

When I am lying in a hammock in a friend's garden looking out over Los Angeles, seeing how the city is enveloped in visible fumes, but at the same time feeling how the sun is doing my body good—it is then that I know that I am *alive*. This is also reality.

As real as when I am sitting here and the snow has melted and Linn is wheeling our black-and-white kitten about.

I think of my sudden breakthrough as a star in America. Unexpected and for me still inexplicable. I don't know if it has made me happier. Whether I feel myself threatened as a professional or, perhaps more importantly, as a woman.

A few months ago I was in California and they spoiled me, as if I were a princess in one of Linn's fairy tales—or myself in one of my childhood dreams. I was surrounded on all sides with kindness and helpfulness. No one allowed me to do anything that was tiring or boring. Always around me were people who wanted to lighten any burdens. At times because they were paid to do so, owned a percentage of me or had invested in my future possibilities. But more often I felt the helpfulness came from goodness.

I was there for three days and then escorted to the airport. At last I was alone, with an armful of roses and good wishes. I had been happy for three days—yet I was glad to be going home again.

I don't altogether trust that life, can be tempted to exchange my soul for honors and fame, seeking admiration, and trading on my charm. I know that today it is still possible to invest in my talent and my personality. But what's going to happen when I become too old? When I am no longer a desirable commodity? When it becomes quiet around me?

The subsequent emptiness is so enormous, for those who choose to live and die in the glare of the arc lights. The loneliness becomes unbearable, because it is in such contrast to that which was.

Beverly Hills. They have sunshine, fresh orange juice,

money, beautiful houses, expensive cars. Simple, ordinary people move into great enclosed fortresses which they call home. Often they don't even know what their neighbors look like. You don't see anyone strolling along the sidewalks in the most elegant residential districts. A summer's day is never greeted by playing children. There are only cars, blinds pulled down to exclude the sun and prying eyes. Gardeners bending in front of the houses tending lawns that no one will sit on.

Nonetheless, there is so much to love: a friendliness and generosity the like of which I have found in few other places in the world. A love of one's profession, a living history of film. One can still meet the historic figures at a party. There is an atmosphere of earlier days still to be felt in the studios and the conversations.

Some of my best and most lasting friends I found when I came to Hollywood to become a star.

I am sitting in a garden outside a small Norwegian town called Strommen. My stomach is full of homemade waffles and as my eyes close by the sunlit wall, I feel that somehow I have been gifted with the best of two worlds.

And in addition I may have seen a good deal of unreality. But that, too, is an experience.

"WHAT IS YOUR STRONGEST HAPPINESS?" I SAY TO A MAN for whom I care. We are in the new summer cottage. Rain is pouring down from a sky that is drearily gray. I had imagined us walking about naked and brown and beautiful and discovering new things from each other in the sun.

"My happiness?" he replies, and looks up from what he is reading. He does not know what I am thinking. Perhaps he is afraid he might not say what I expect to hear.

"My happiness—I think it is when I have worked in the sweat of my body a whole day on something hard and physical. When I've had to use my entire body, when I've become exhausted and my limbs are aching—and then finally I finish. Come in and sit down. Rest in the knowledge that I've achieved what I set out to do. Relax in the joy of a job well done."

He does not ask what my happiness is. But the next day I know. We have had a sumptuous lunch. He praises my cooking and takes several helpings. And we lie on the bed and are close. Sated with tenderness. When we no longer have any fears or questions between us. Only tender pleasure in the other's body and hands and face and expression. I am together with him, in the only way that I really *live*.

When I awake and it is still light outside, he is gone, and I go with bare feet into the living room, still warm and happy from him, and see that he has lit the fireplace. In the kitchen I find coffee he has put on the hot plate for me, with a cup beside it.

I have not a thread on my body as I go out into the garden.

It is still raining and toes slide into earth that is wet and fragrant. And then I see him down by the garage splitting wood so that I shall have enough for the winter. He has made a chopping block and bought an ax for the house. I don't know what he is thinking, but he looks so happy and brown and alive. Suddenly I remember that he is in the middle of his happiness.

And I go in again and feel *my* happiness flowing through my whole body.

ONE DAY LINN AND I RETURN TO THE ISLAND WHERE WE lived for many years, long, long ago.

Linn is going to spend the summer with her father and his new wife.

I am only coming for a few days.

First of all to meet Ingmar, but also to see the island once again; feel how much of it is still part of me. Meet people I was close to. See a beloved dog again.

Linn's father meets us at the airport.

It is strange to be back. We drive through the familiar landscape: the flowers . . . the dust along the road . . . the line of tourists at the ferry slip . . . a somewhat rough crossing . . . the landscape more barren . . . fewer and fewer cars.

Finally it is only us on a forest road which almost no one knows about.

"Welcome back," he says, and smiles.

Linn jumps out of the car before we are home to see if she can find some wild strawberries.

Ingrid, the wife, stands in the doorway. She is tan and happy; her hair is long and kept together with a ribbon. I can see that she resembles another woman who once stood in that doorway and waited for guests.

A little knot in the stomach.

I also see that she is more secure than the other, more serene. That is good to know. Linn loves to come here, partly because of her.

"You are going to stay in the guest house," she says. "We have looked forward so much to your visit. I have bought champagne."

My throat tightens. Why does it affect me more deeply

when *she* says it than when he said the same thing in the car?
I know that I shall never be able to express to her how grateful I am, not only that I sense his close friendship, but also for
her having made it possible for me to return to a place that for
a long time was *my* home.

Nothing is changed. Even the furniture is arranged as before.

The circle is closed.

Nothing ever comes to an end. Wherever one has sunk
roots that emanate from one's best or truest self, one will
always find a home.

To return is not to revisit something that has failed. I can
walk along the old paths without bitterness that other feet are
now taking pleasure in them.

The sea is there just as it always has been.

I can sit down at the dinner table and use the knives and
forks and glasses that once were bought by me, and feel a bit
sad, but at the same time know I am still a part of this house
—one of its close friends.

I am moved by the fact that so little has changed, and I like
her for that. She has not tried to remove me from this place.

Ingmar is here.

People whose lives have touched need to renew contact,
even when they have gone in different directions. Even when
their new lives are a part of what they now share.

No one owns anyone. Together, we have each other and
nature and time.

It is as simple as that.

We bring the suitcases to the guest cottage. From the window I can look down at the main house. I have never seen it
from here, and it is rather strange, but my inner being is
calm.

Nothing can hurt me anymore.

ISLANDERS

So much has been written about our life at Fårö. People who have never been there and never known us have written chapters.

But I remain dumb when someone asks me to talk about it.

I was young and had so many ideas about what life should be.

Pictures—which are fragments of our life together: walks on the beach, when like children we buried coins in the sand so that we could find them again many years later. In case we were poor or war had come. A small pile of stones in memory of a summer day and of two people who knew how to play together.

Nights, when we lay close to each other and he whispered that I must be quiet, so that he, in the stillness, could long for me and ask me to talk to him again.

Our boundless need for each other, for what the other one should represent. The powerlessness when something went wrong.

We entered into each other's lives too early and too late.

I sought the absolute security, protection. A great need to belong.

He sought the mother. Arms that would open to him, warm and without complications.

Perhaps our love originated in the loneliness we both had known before.

His dream was the woman who had been created in one piece. But I crumbled into all kinds of bits and pieces if he wasn't careful.

When we had parted, we clearly saw the mistakes we had made.

His hunger for togetherness was insatiable. That hunger became a vital necessity for me.

In a way each seeded a revolution in the other. We opened to each other so completely. Not only physically, not only sexually—but like human beings related in a secret way, we bound ourselves together.

After a short time I was confronted with his jealousy. Violent and without bounds. I had never experienced such a thing before. Now all doors were closed, barred. Friends and family, even memories, became a threat to our relationship. Terrified, I felt I only had *him*. And when his jealousy had placed limits on my freedom, I entered into his territory, in order to create the same limits there for him. Experienced my own security only as far as I could control his life.

We longed to have no secrets from each other. We yearned for the courage to surrender ourselves. But when it finally happened, we were no longer living together.

Our needs were impossible to satisfy.

That became our hell. Our drama.

There was a door in his study, which we covered with hearts and crosses and tears and black rings. Symbols of what we had been to each other that day.

Nothing existed outside ourselves. No joy or pain that had not been inflicted by the other.

Slowly this became the grounds for the breakup.

We were so much alike. What he had not known about himself he began to see in me—as if in a mirror—despite the fact that I was a woman and much younger and perhaps unlike him in ways that he didn't know. He saw his own vulnerability and his own anger in me. And when this was reflected back at him, he began to be healed. But like a mirror, I was always there as a reminder.

I wanted to be his, and if he had wanted me to change, I

would have done anything. Maybe it is possible to change together—develop together. But if the mirror is too clear, one will not only see oneself as one *is*, one will also be forced to leave that other person who will always be a reminder of what one no longer wishes to be.

THE FIRST SUMMER WAS PURE HAPPINESS.

We were making *Persona* on the island.

It was hot. I was experiencing another human being. He was experiencing me. And we didn't need to talk about it. I was barefoot in sand so fine it felt as if it breathed beneath my feet.

During the day I would lie on the ground and read between takes. And my head felt heavy, almost as if I were unconscious.

I never wondered what might come of our relationship. It was as if I were living within soft walls of sunlight and desire and happiness.

No summer since has ever been like that. Not like that. We went for walks along the shore and never spoke, made no demands, were not afraid.

Once we wandered far from the others, discovered a small ridge of gray stones with barren, unfertile earth beyond. We sat and looked at the sea, which for once lay completely still in the sunlight.

He took my hand in his and said:

"I had a dream last night. That you and I are painfully connected."

On the spot where we were sitting he built his house.

And that changed his life. And mine.

The next time I saw the island it was winter. He brought me there in a small private plane. What was to become our home was already being built. Together we were to see it for the first time.

The meeting with the summer paradise was a shock. I saw a completely new landscape. The cold penetrated the body. One could not defend oneself.

I had been through a divorce which hurt; left a person I was fond of.

Ingmar and I had a daughter together.

Everything was different.

The house was located far away from the sandy beach of summer, the site was all stone and dry earth. No one on the island could understand the man who had bought so much infertile land.

We entered underneath the thin scaffolding into the skeleton of our home.

Someone had brought champagne and I broke the bottle and we made speeches and christened the house.

We walked on the beach, which was nothing but rocks, and took pictures of each other. I look happy in all of them, but I know that I was thinking: This is a dream. I'm taking part in someone else's dream.

All that had formerly been my life was unreal and far away.

Yet this, too, was strange to me.

I wondered what would become of me.

BIBI ANDERSSON AND I PLAYED THE MAIN ROLES IN *Persona*. Bibi's character talked and cried and raged throughout the movie.

My only line was: "Nothing."

It was the first time I met a film director who let me unveil feelings and thoughts no one else had recognized. A director who listened patiently, his index finger to his temple, and who understood everything I was trying to express. A genius who created an atmosphere in which everything could happen— even that which I had not known about myself.

Most of the picture was filmed at Fårö. We stayed in a small house—the make-up artist, the script girl, Bibi and I. Our landlady spoiled us. Every morning there were several hot dishes at breakfast, until Bibi and I had to protest as we swelled into round and pudgy girls instead of the slim ones we had been when the picture started in Stockholm.

Under big hats to protect our faces against the sun, we spent the days sitting studying our scripts and displayed a private happiness that was never seen in the movie. Although—once—directly out of our reality, two women sit cleaning mushrooms, each humming a different melody. It is Alma and Elisabeth Vogler of *Persona*; but it is also Bibi and Liv, 1965.

We were both newly married when we met for the first time on an island off northern Norway. Sandrewfilm was making a film of Knut Hamsun's *Pan*, and wanted to feature a well-known actress from each of the neighboring countries. Bibi's part was much larger than mine, and her film experience more extensive. We shared a classroom in the school, which was closed for the summer. We pushed all the desks into a heap up toward the blackboard, and placed our beds at angles in a corner. There we were lying with an enormous floor space and a pile of stacked chairs and tables between ourselves and the door. We talked all night long. There was the midnight sun and a lot to tell each other. Later on in life we would sleep.

We pictured the future, our marriages, our childhood and youth, and promised to be godmothers to each other's children.

I admired her for her generosity and her honesty.

The ties between us became stronger than those I had had with any other woman friend, and through the years the friendship has endured.

One day she received a telegram from Ingmar Bergman. I looked at her in wonder because she was so calm. She folded it up and was going to put it in her handbag. I asked her if I could keep it.

Now the three of us were making *Persona* on Fårö.

Bibi had a premonition of what would happen, and she spoke to me sternly but completely in vain. I looked at her from the distant heaven where I resided in my capacity as the first woman on earth who loved and was loved.

In the evenings we took walks along the beach—Bibi, Sven Nykvist, the photographer, Ingmar and I. In spite of her warnings, Bibi's girlfriend loyalty won out and she would turn toward Sven and shout, "Race you home." Sven had to run along the beach evening after evening, in mild wonder at Bibi's enormous and sudden energy.

While Ingmar and I followed slowly.

Every night when I came home I was confronted by a big black cat sitting by the door and watching me maliciously.

I tiptoed in to Bibi, and sat curled on her bed and whispered all that I had not been able to tell him.

THE ISLAND LIES BETWEEN RUSSIA AND SWEDEN.
I could not remember having seen a place so barren. Like a relic from the Stone Age. But in the summer sunlight, moving and rather mysterious.

At night we could see the ocean from our bedroom. And we imagined ourselves passengers on a journey. Lights from ships in the far, far distance we looked upon as mysterious messages to strangers down on our beach. We pretended we were in constant danger, because the house was so isolated and we only had each other.

When I was a girl I dreamed of another kind of island. It had palm trees and fruits and warmth. And when it was night there, the animals of the forest kept watch over me. I never associated loneliness and eeriness with that.

His island had gnarled spruce trees of strange green colors, most of them stunted and bent along the ground. Only the strongest managed to lift themselves upward. And when the dusk came, they looked, in their vain longing toward heaven, like slender female dancers no longer able to stand on their toes.

The most beautiful of all the trees grew outside our living-room window, and he told me it was mine. The winter after I left the island, it blew down. That made me happy. He could not share it with somebody else.

The ground was gray and brown—wide fields covered by dry moss. One month every summer the whole island burst into the most wonderful colors. It reminded me of the flower fields of my childhood. And when we went picking wild strawberries together we were happy. But when the days got short and the colors more subdued and difficult to discern, the island became a prison in which I didn't know where to go with my loneliness and insecurity. I was anxious the whole time and longed for other places. But I never told anyone.

At the same time I knew that I had never been closer to life.

The brief glimpses of happiness marked me more than anything I had previously experienced. And whatever was painful and difficult to understand paved the way for the inner change which I unconsciously was longing for.

Along the island's shoreline there ran a belt of stones, miles of stones washed by the sea. In only one place the stones gave way to sand and became a beach that lured thousands of tourists every summer.

When they arrived we became more isolated. We looked forward to the day when the ferries once more would cross the sound empty and we would no longer need to glance up at the brick wall he had built around the house, to see whether anyone was standing there with a camera: making us strangers and powerless in our own garden.

I knew that Ingmar had found his island, and I tried to love it the way he did.

On the nights when he couldn't sleep, I would lie silent beside him, afraid of what he was thinking. Perhaps that I was not a part of the island—that I disturbed the harmony he tried to create within himself in the nature and the stillness that meant so much to him.

My security became living the way he wished. For only then was *he* secure.

I HAD A DOG BY THE NAME OF PET.

In her first home, with Jappe, she was gentle and affectionate. She loved to lie in his lap, and if she had been a cat she would have purred.

When my husband came home from the hospital, she could recognize the sound of his car from her place on the sofa on the fourth floor. A small pointed head looked eagerly out of the window and everyone within a mile's radius could hear her loud yelps of joy. Then followed a feast of endearment between dog and man.

When we ate she would lie at her master's feet and look up at him adoringly.

Then Ingmar came into her life, and the distrust was great on both sides. He attempted to bribe my friends to help him get rid of Pet. He asked them to take her into a street with heavy traffic, send her on to a final sleep at the veterinarian, leave her behind at the opposite end of town. But no one would.

He and she chased each other wildly around my apartment. One of them kicked, the other bit. I was never again allowed to pat her or in any other way show her attention when *he* was there, and *she* growled when Ingmar took my hand.

When I moved to Fårö, Pet came along and was a very unwelcome guest.

She was given a small closet in the kitchen passageway to sleep in. The living room was off limits. We had to steal our caresses when *he* was on the beach or in his study.

But she was so smart that she very soon understood it was best to give love to the person who evidently was in command of her destiny.

And slowly Pet manipulated her way into the living room.

One yard per day, until finally she occupied a flattering position by the big open fireplace.

Never has a dog expressed such a degree of understanding
as when Ingmar read aloud to me from a script. She looked
dreamily into the air when his favorite records were being
played. Her entire body quivered with longing when he put
on his overcoat to take a walk, and she jumped for joy when
she was finally given permission to go along, barking and
bounding about in a violent demonstration, so that he would
understand how important it was to take a watchdog along
when strolling on the beach.

"Pet is an emotion on four legs," Ingmar said.

When I left the house five years later, the two of them
were standing together in the doorway. Pet sniffed at the
ground, so perhaps she was a bit ashamed of her betrayal.

Now I hear that in her fifteenth year, she lies on his desk
while new scripts are being written. And I would not be surprised if her vain brain harbors dreams of immortality in one
of his films.

I was searching for something on an island.

Here people lived close to the earth, close to the sea, close to that which is natural and predetermined for us.

The distinctive mark of the people I met, when the tourists had left at the end of summer, was their simplicity.

None of these men and women, I felt, could ever be humbled. They lived in harmony with their own selves, with everything that was good and evil in them. No outsiders could point at them and make them feel inferior.

People who had trust in their place on earth. They were far from uncomplicated, nor without demands, hatreds and aggressions. But they had pride, a dignity which they allowed no one to crush. They had roots which had been lodged in the same piece of earth their entire lives.

Many old people have that. They have renounced pretensions, dropped the false dream, stopped the mad rush.

They, too, are islanders in our society.

The way children are.

People who don't care to keep the mask and the façade in order. Who dare to show who they are.

Islanders.

The ones who live their thoughts. Even thoughts that may not be so remarkable.

From some of them emanates a feeling of security, a feeling of simple security, which may be the dignity of the heart.

Siri had lived on the island her entire life. Only once had she been to Stockholm and the fear was still with her. Her behind was big and broad, as if at the end of a working day she had sat a lot. Sat and pondered.

When still a young girl she was charged with the responsibility for her orphaned brothers and sisters. Not until the last one left home did she have time to think about herself and what she wanted to do with her life.

Further schooling was out of the question. Besides, she was no longer that young. And she was a woman.

She remained on the island and took odd jobs whenever a woman's labor was needed. She was able to keep her parents' little farm and what work came with it.

She gave birth to a child and raised it alone. Several years later a man moved in with her. A silent and tender friendship bound them together.

She was beautiful. Large features with deep, heavy-set eyes. Breasts and hips full of womanliness and motherliness.

When *we* came to the island, *she* came to us.

Every day she rode through the woods on her old bicycle. Even when Ingmar gave her a scooter, she felt safer on the unsteady vehicle from her youth. She wondered at the life we were living, but was also understanding and full of tenderness. When we sat at the dinner table and were all nerves and unspoken words, she would stare from one to the other, and then bend over her plate, quite unable to understand why two would hurt each other who were so in love. At times she stayed in the kitchen crying because she had so completely identified herself with a situation to which she was a stranger.

If we were happy, she would be happier than we.

She winked at me and smiled and would almost lose her fear of the dark when she biked home in the evening.

We understood each other, the way women do when they allow intimacy.

She gave me insight into much that previously had not been within my world: what a working day is when one owns sheep and chickens and geese and some land, and in addition works as a maid and substitutes as a salesgirl in the grocery store. From me, she learned something from other countries, from travels—from the life outside the island. We sat hand in hand or with arms around each other's waists. Felt happy for the experiences we shared, cried at times because the other suddenly understood something one had been alone with earlier.

We went to the island celebrations together. First we would look through our dresses and help each other select the finest one for the evening.

The men would sit in a corner and talk while the women danced, as is often the custom in the country.

I danced with Siri and I danced with Rosa, one forty, the other sixty years old. Siri in her silk dress, tight on a good strong body which now was filled with happiness.

The daily pattern was abandoned for a few hours. Today when I think of them my mouth smiles—the same way it did that evening.

She did not read much, did not watch the same television programs I did, but she was in many ways more closely tied to reality than I was.

Her responsibility had always been to others, the reward in material things very small. She was proud and dignified. Locked in a room, I would rather spend a hundred days with her than with certain people I know, renowned for their wit and intellect.

I miss Siri, now that I never see her anymore.

THE SHEEP ON THE ISLAND STAY OUT OF DOORS ALL YEAR. Like the landscape on which they live, they look like survivors from another time. Curiously shaped heads, big bodies heavy with wool that drags along the ground.

When they give birth in March, the temperature may be 30 degrees below zero.

One day we stood completely helpless and watched the process. The wind lashed our faces. It was dark and stormy. A lamb was hanging from the mother's body while she stood waiting, her head bowed to the wind. Life was of short duration for the little one. It was no sooner born and the mother's tongue had touched it than a second lamb arrived. And it was the survival of the fittest. The mother began licking the last arrival, which was considerably larger. The small one remained lying on the ground, while blood and slime turned to ice on its body.

We made an awkward attempt to help, but only succeeded in frightening the mother away, and we had to withdraw. Cautiously she came back to her biggest child and licked it until, dry and on thin and wobbly legs, it rose to test the world.

That evening the farmer collected three dead lambs the flock had left behind as they continued their slow trek through the evergreen forest.

A LITTLE CHILD GREW UP WITH US ON THE ISLAND.
I stood in the hospital corridor the night after she was born.
Through a window I could see all the small, crying newborn
infants, and somewhere among them slept the one who was
mine. I stood there for hours filled with happiness, until a
night nurse sent me to bed.

How can I explain the enormous feeling of security in
knowing that now she was with me in the world? Soon her
bed would stand next to mine. We would fall asleep hand in
hand. We would listen to music and look at beautiful pictures
together. We would discuss everything in life, and find the
answers in long confidential conversations. Linn and I would
help each other be real people. I felt even then that it would
be only the two of us. That Linn's father had to live his own
life, near us—but never with us. I lay in my bed and twisted
the ring he had given me, put on the light to admire it. Read
the letter he had written to his daughter and me. No danger
in the world could reach me this first night.

Dreams seldom become reality.

I was to give a child security and tenderness, but didn't feel
I received enough of this myself. In the loneliness on the
island I was often a nervous and short-tempered mother. My
life with the child was influenced by the situation I found
myself in, and it was not always a good one. My disappoint-
ments at times worked themselves out on her. There were
days with guilt feelings when I became the doormat for both
of them. He who sat in his study and wanted to own me
alone. And she who could barely walk, and cried for me from
the other end of the house. I rushed from one to the other,
always with a bad conscience. Never able to completely give
what I yearned to receive.

There are many pictures of Linn from that time. She is chubby and happy; her eyes look as if they already appraise everything that happens around her. Eyes full of humor.

I know I can never make amends for the wrongs I have done her. All the choices I made that were not to her advantage. Every time I left her in someone else's care.

I wonder what she was thinking, what she was longing for.

I want to take her in my lap today and tell her how much I love her and how I miss the warmth and the smell and the absolute trust.

The time when I was her entire world and was filled with my own. When she slept in one end of the house and we in the other. And I lay listening because she was so far away that I was afraid I would not hear if she woke.

The blue crib. The picture of Ingmar as a boy above it.

Moments of belonging when we walked in the woods and picked strawberries. When it thundered so terribly one night, and we all three lay close together in bed and laughed.

My happiness when the two of them locked themselves into his study and had secrets. Summer days when we sat outside the house and were completely quiet, looking at the sea and the birds and the stones.

The first years of her life she lived there with us. And she has already forgotten most of it.

What memories and experiences lie buried deep within her and will place their stamp on her in later life? Will bring to her fears and insecurity that she will never understand? Longings that can never be fulfilled? Because they belonged to an early childhood and could only have been satisfied at that time.

I HAVE A SCHOOL PICTURE OF INGMAR. HE IS STANDING IN the middle of a row of thirteen-year-old boys. I can see that his skin is pimply, recognize the loneliness and the bashfulness, and believe I can sense his feeling of being an outsider.

Once we were invited to dinner by a rich producer in Rome. We were supposed to be the only guests, but within half an hour the host's large apartment was filled with people who had been invited to meet Ingmar at close range. Then he had the same expression as in that picture. He was pale when he told the producer he had to leave at once. The others sat down for dinner without the guest of honor.

Every afternoon Linn and he and I would take the Fårö ferry across the sound to fetch the newspapers. Often on the way home we would buy ice cream. Even in winter when it was storming and people wore woolen scarves and red noses— we would sit in the car eating ice cream.

One Christmas on the island I bought smoked, salted ham thinking it was fresh, roasted it for an hour and served up an inedible catastrophe. Later that evening I tried to light some candles on the veranda. The wind blew out the flickering flames and Ingmar tapped angrily on the window, because I had mistakenly bought funeral candles, thinking they were party ones.

Filming on Fårö. He had been angry with me since breakfast. I was standing in front of a blazing house. "Closer," he shouted, peering into the camera. Sparks were flying round my ears. "Closer!" The heat on my face was so fierce I had to close my eyes. I was full of hate. "Closer!" I was on my way into the inferno before he called, "That's enough!" But on the screen it looks good.

In Rome I had one great wish: to walk into a bar and drink

fresh orange juice at the counter. I persuaded him to follow me inside. He stood by the door, furious. People crowded together and against him in the cramped quarters. He had to wait because I was standing in line. The juice didn't taste as good as I had imagined and when we were outside again, he told me it was the last time he would ever be lured into such an adventure.

For five weeks we ate at the same restaurant.

We went to St. Peter's every day. We loved to stroll about in the wonderful light, and the dark and the colors and the shadows and the cool inside the cathedral. We sat on a bench and promised each other to return to the same place another year.

I came back—but it was Linn who was with me.

"Here Papa and I once sat when you were a little baby," I told her wistfully.

"Many bottoms have sat here since yours," Linn retorted dryly.

The gardens above the Roman Forum. Never before had we seen spring in this way. Speechless with pleasure, we looked at the orange trees and the palms, walked in the shadow of a sun that was warmer than the one we had at home in the summer.

No one could be as angry as Ingmar. Possibly I.

Once I was so frightened of him that I locked myself in the bathroom. He stood outside hammering and kicking at the door trying to get in. Suddenly to my horror I saw his whole foot come through the door like a cannon ball, leaving a large hole—and with such a force that his slipper came off and flew into the bowl.

It was easy to become friends again when we could see ourselves from the outside.

As when he, in a rage, pushed me right across the hotel room, knocking a new hat down over my face, where it stuck, effectively closing off any protest for a while.

We were seldom bored together. I remember once in the zoological garden. We looked at the animals and walked and walked and looked at animals and had nothing to talk about. Even though it was sunny and hot. Afterward we drank cocoa in a restaurant. We were both glad when the walk was over and we could sit down, each with an evening paper.

Or in Copenhagen once. We had looked forward for so long to being alone together. For several days we saw no one, and one afternoon we stood looking out of the hotel window. An emptiness materialized between us, wordless and completely unexpected.

We went to sleep with our foreheads touching. Like horses.

When we were to make our first journey together, he sent me ahead with all the luggage, so that I could unpack and make the hotel room like home by the time he arrived. The violent protest inside me finally exploded after several days, and in the middle of the night I suddenly announced that we had reached the end of our relationship and it would be just as well if he got up and ordered himself a new room. Exceedingly slowly, he dressed. For minutes he stood in front of the mirror combing his thinning hair. He looked like the boy in the school photograph.

When he and Fellini met, they were brothers within an instant. They embraced, laughed together as if they had lived the same life. They wandered through the streets in the night, arms around each other, Fellini wearing a dramatic black cape, Ingmar in his little cap and an old winter coat.

Dinner at Fellini's house, when Ingmar sat in a corner with Giulietta Masina, Fellini's wife, and she lost her shyness and started to sing. A high, clear voice, like a child's.

"I can't leave the room for a moment without my wife making a fool of herself," Fellini said in the doorway. She got up quickly. Did not answer. Through the veranda window I could see her walking in the garden, picking blossoms from the trees. Later she came in again and gave us one each. She smiled the whole time.

But when she moved, it was on tiptoe—so that no one would notice her.

Ingmar and I had an arrangement whereby at his funeral I should appear in a long, black dress. I should have preferred red. And if he was married to someone else, I would go and take my place at the back of the church after everyone else had arrived, faint during the eulogy and be carried out during the recessional.

A year after our break I was sitting on the steps of St. Peter's. The sun was shining and I was a little in love. All at once I felt that from then on Rome would hold other memories than Ingmar.

And I wrote him a letter saying that it was all over.

IT IS A SHORT LOVE STORY THAT RESEMBLES SO MANY others.

It lasted five years.

When she had lived with him for a few years she began to observe him. She would sit quietly and experience him as an individual.

One who no longer existed only in relation to her.

Gradually, within her an understanding of him awakened. The more he retreated from her, the better she understood him—as if the distance gave her clarity.

The fear diminished and the loneliness was easier to bear when she saw his insecurity.

She would become filled with tenderness and look beyond his violence and his injustice.

She was no longer blind to his faults and weaknesses, as she had been at the beginning. But her understanding and respect for him grew.

The adoration disappeared. She noticed that his hair was gray; he was much older than she; he was wise and stimulating; he was vain and egotistical.

And she discovered to her surprise that this was love.

With sadness she realized that it would soon be over, that she had come to him when he was already on his way somewhere else.

She looked at their child and realized that she would soon have that responsibility alone.

The last year she fought for their relationship, even though she knew it was hopeless, and not right for either of them.

And when it was all over she hoped that he would not be alone.

That the new woman would take better care of him than she had.

But of course it took her some time to reach that point.

She tried to recall who she had been when she came to the island five years before.

Something had been crushed in her, and something was more alive.

She had undergone a change.

And when bitterness and hate and despair were gone, she was sure she had experienced love and been enriched.

But she would never be able to talk about it.

She had seen into another person and was full of tenderness for what she had found.

For a period of time they had taken each other's hands and been painfully connected.

But only when it was all over did they become true friends.

EVERYTHING THAT WAS FAMILIAR TO ME WAS MANY MILES away—people, fragrances, sounds, experiences. Here, on the island, I was in a strange world with strange trees and stones. Colors that only gradually revealed themselves.

I was cut off from everything that earlier had been my life. And I was in the process of searching for a new life within myself.

A change made possible by the loneliness on his island.

When I cried, stormed against him, when he shut himself in his study, when he left me for a day—while it was all very painful, I knew that it did help me develop.

I had always followed others because I was insecure. I was accustomed to reach for the hands of others for help and understanding.

But now when I was more afraid and more alone than ever, I achieved for the first time a sense of security with myself.

And I longed for the man who sat writing in his study. I wanted to share with him this new knowledge, but I couldn't.

I walked on the stony beach and imagined I was a part of the nature of the island, and that I would always live here.

I tried to love the turbulent sea, the strange colors that released their beauty so frugally.

And the more I tried, the more frightened I became that I would not be living there much longer.

I wanted to open my arms and embrace it all, but because my fear that it would never be mine was so great, it never became mine.

I lived there for a brief period of my life, and what I brought away with me was not the stones and the trees and the beauty.

I left the island with loneliness in my baggage, and the feeling that something inside me had changed forever.

WHAT IS THERE TO TELL ABOUT THE ACTUAL DEPARTURE?
The publicity around the private grief? The newspapers
that pushed into our lives. Stomped on what was painful.
Magazines with cover pictures from our first times together.
Smiling and happy faces with black captions: "HIS NEW LIFE
WITHOUT LIV. READ THE END OF THE STORY." In our misery
we were on an intimate footing with half of Scandinavia.

A reporter called in friendly commiseration and said that I
could choose to tell the truth myself, or else place the press in
such a position that they would have to write their own version. Another asked if I had the telephone number of his new
woman.

I had to sneak out of a hotel room and run down the back
stairs because there were photographers waiting at the main
entrance. Dark glasses to conceal a grief—a little human
suffering running by in a picture makes for good sales. Especially when the text furnishes an intimate account of disaster.

I remember standing in a back alley among garbage cans
and laundry lines, waiting for a car. In my dramatic way I
experienced the situation symbolically and decided that I
couldn't spend the rest of my life like this. Among garbage
cans.

I remember friends waiting at the airport when I arrived in
Sweden right afterward. I was frightened and shy before all
the looks and remarks. The girls had champagne and placards.
They were standing in hippie fashion, waving their texts
which said: "LIFE GOES ON." "WELCOME LIV."

I laughed for the first time in ages and spilled champagne
on the terminal floor.

We stayed up all night at Bibi's house. Four or five women,
each with a love story to relate. Each with a place, somewhere
on earth, where they could no longer return.

As long as we lived on the island together it was the practical matters one had to consider in order to break out. It was very complicated for the one who suddenly had to leave, and that was always me.

First, I had to drive through three or four gates, which all had to be opened and closed: leave the car—open the gate—drive through—out again and close it. Then there was the ferry. It left once an hour, and our fights never coincided with its schedule. When I finally had crossed the sound, it was still an hour's drive to the airport. By the time I got there my anger was gone and I always turned around and went back.

Often he would be standing waiting for me by one of the gates.

We were so childish, the two of us.

Once when we were really furious at each other and decided that we couldn't risk the complicated exit from the island, he called for a taxiplane, which was to land at the ferry dock. So that it wouldn't be too embarrassing sitting next to the pilot in case he understood, in case I cried, Ingmar explained over the telephone that I had to leave in a hurry, because my grandmother was seriously ill. I began to pack in a great hurry and he sat on a chair watching with that faint smile of his. The one from the photograph—the school picture.

We became friends again, there by the suitcases.

When we remembered the plane, he called and told them to return to Stockholm: Grandmother had made a speedy recovery.

When the final separation came, we didn't talk about it. We pretended that it had no meaning when I packed all my clothes. Just a short visit to Norway.

Linn's things were left behind. Those I didn't dare touch—
it would have been too obvious, too final.

I didn't look back as the car drove away, leaving behind all
that we had found together—chairs and lamps and tables.
The view and the sounds of the sea and the trees.

Siri, who understood everything better than we, stood behind the curtain and cried.

But we didn't cry. Not then.

You cannot imagine how much we hoped in the beginning.

As LONG AS I LIVED ON THE ISLAND, I KEPT THINKING that I would be able to break through the isolation and find him on the other side.

We recognized so much in each other. Perhaps we were too much alike.

Sometimes he said that we were.

I used to dream about a great togetherness and was sure that we could achieve it.

But with the break came the final isolation—and I knew it would never happen.

And then something broke inside me.

The girl within me wept and wept. She made all of me, who after all was thirty, into a little thirteen-year-old again.

Until I had no more tears and realized it was impossible to live as if my life could only be fulfilled through another person. Pointless to seek refuge in someone else from what was *my* loneliness and insecurity.

Ingmar was no longer in my life as before. That was a fact, and nothing could alter it.

But I still had myself, contact with my own being, everything in me that wanted to continue onward.

I missed Ingmar's daily presence, but I knew I had his friendship and it was up to me, who at that moment needed it most, to find a new point of contact at which we could both meet.

With all the power I owned, I built a bridge between us, and after that everything was better.

For a time we used to phone each other several times a day. I read him pieces of my old compositions. He played me his favorite records.

Love has many faces.

I made better contact with others. I found respect when I became independent, ceased to cling. Ceased to rely so desperately on others for my own happiness.

Demands and expectations on other people's behavior, in order to make me secure, vanished. Not quite. Not forever. But I never reverted to the old state.

Sorrow turned—if you like—into joy.

I think some experiences are less frequent now, but I live a more harmonious life.

That is how it works for me.

I believe that the overpowering happiness—when the whole world is fragrant and the sun shines and one is almost unconscious from emotion—I believe it comes less frequently.

But it exists. I shall always be aware that it exists. However, I do not worry because it is not part of my daily life.

I no longer believe in a constant state of happiness. How does one measure happiness?

I think it is good to recognize what the moment is about and accept it as a gift.

I give birth to a child for the first time. This boundless event I shall never have again, but it enhances everything I shall later feel.

I sit by the light of a candle and believe I never would perceive the flickering flame as I do if I had not at one time seen Linn come into the world.

I left Fårö and my roots were never allowed to take hold in the earth, but they are forever planted in the experiences the island gave me.

Gifts are not happiness only. I think I accept that.

I believe this is my most important change.

TWINKLE, TWINKLE, LITTLE STAR

THE FIRST WINTER WAS DIFFICULT. LIKE GOING BACK IN time and finding everything awaiting me which I had left behind. It was also happiness to know that the change was not an obstacle—I could continue from where I was when I left Norway five years earlier. Or in the beginning was that just something I thought? My colleagues at the National Theatre said "Hi" and looked at me as if I had been there all the time. Though that might have been something I imagined.

Linn's playmates, whom she had seen only occasionally, now came regularly to our home. The house I bought while I was still married functioned as I had dreamed it would. Neighbors chatting across the fence or ringing at the door and sitting by the kitchen table with a cup of coffee. The faucets leaked and the fuses blew; I had to learn how to do all sorts of practical things—and I was proud when I made things work. All was normal. Here I had been thinking that the end of the world had come. And then I was again in my old bed as if nothing had happened.

It is Sunday morning and my four-year-old is in the living room talking on the telephone with her father. Outside, it is dark and snowing. Soon I shall get up and light a few candles, get the fire going, and have breakfast with Linn, as I imagine all other mothers are doing at this moment with their children.

I shall be a troll and a bear, and play with greater pleasure and involvement than during the week after returning from long rehearsals of Racine's *Britannicus* at the theatre.

Linn is having a lively discussion with Ingmar. She wants him to crawl through the telephone and visit her.

I cry at times.

Linn suddenly stands in the doorway:

"Why are you crying, Mamma?"

"Sometimes I feel a bit lonely."

"You have me!"

"But grownups need other grownups as well."

"You have Granny and Aunt Nan."

"Once in a while you long for a person who will look after you."

"Well, you have the one on Fårö."

Linn opens the curtains and shuts the window.

"If you get up now, Mamma, you may tell me how children are made."

It is not only the morning that is long on a Sunday—the whole day is endless. In both good and bad.

The rest of the week passes quickly. Voice lessons every morning. My teacher is eager and happy, uses her whole body to demonstrate, runs up the stairs ahead of me, sings herself when she can no longer bear to listen to me. She is seventy-eight, and I am always in high spirits when I leave her.

In the theatre it's the other way around. They are all good-looking and able except me. I am making such an effort, but the stanzas are too long and the form too rigid. I can never get anywhere near the young girl, Junia, whom Racine has described. What a strange part to give me. After all, I am thirty, filled with experience I long to use, and now I am to be squeezed into the limitations of an eighteen-year-old ingénue. The result is a clodhopper from Trondhjem sneaking onto the stage hoping not to be noticed. I still have received no salary. I feel a stranger and somewhat unwelcome.

My work on radio is far more significant for me: I am playing Nora in *A Doll's House*. Into her farewell I try to put a slight hope of reunion. My own departure is still so recent.

I wonder how many Noras there are in the world who would *like* to go, but never dare. And if they go—where? Is it important to know—or is it the actual step through the door that counts? The will to meet the world beyond one's own constructed security.

The evenings are all like one another. Sometimes I go out with friends, but I prefer to stay home with Linn. We have our rituals. We take a bath together, read together, watch television together. I must say the prayers. The last time she did it herself she called upon God in a high childish voice. And then with mounting impatience: "Go-o-od!" Disappointed, she looked at me as if it were my fault, and said, "He does not answer!" Now I say the prayers, while she lies in bed disbelieving and thinking me stupid. But I dare not take chances. She shall have that support, in case He is listening.

The first night of *Britannicus*. Onstage I am two people: one tries to act, the other stands beside, criticizing every movement, every word. At times even sneaks down into the audience and sits on the lap of a skeptical spectator, avidly absorbing the critical thoughts found there. These two people (who are both me) get tangled up together, make me feel sick, and I seriously consider pretending to faint so that the curtain can come down.

In the night my agent phones and tells me I can become an international star, but not if I intend to sit in Oslo. He says I can pick and choose my parts.

A decision slowly forms in the dark. I don't know where meaningful work is to be found. I don't even know exactly what I want. But I am certain I must try something other than what I am doing now.

I feel that change is in the offing.

I FILMED IN ENGLAND AND FRANCE AND DENMARK AND Rumania and Sweden. Linn came with me, and we saw a lot of the world. I no longer had a contract with the theatre. I could no longer make references to my roots at home.

But I had my house which I loved, the books and records, the spruce trees outside, the heather on which Linn could run about barefoot, her dolls' house and the hundred tulips we had planted.

My friends. The family.

We had much to long for from our various hotel rooms. And when I said our prayers at night, I mentioned it all.

We met all sorts of people: famous and stupid and wise and kind and poor and rich.

I sent letters home to Norway saying what fun it was working abroad, yet there were doubts as I wrote.

The thought of being in my own kitchen! I would make tea and fry eggs. Linn would sit at her table, leafing through a picture book.

I used all the money I had saved and bought an old sailing boat. It was moored in an Italian harbor and was to be my roots in the world.

I did not know how to sail, and spent a dreadful week at sea with a friend, during which we were both seasick all the time. When I had to move on, he promised to look after the boat. I never saw it again—he told me someone had stolen it, and bought himself an antique shop. I wrote to Bibi that I had prematurely become the target of gigolos.

One day I was given a lovely poem on homesickness. Sean Connery, who wrote it, also traveled about as I did, spending his nights in strange beds. In his luggage he had a large bundle of writings. He read many of them to me. A suitcase filled with sheets of paper, crumpled and some of them quite smudged. Written on hotel stationery from all over the world. A secret life he carried with him so as not to be a stranger on earth. He told me of his longing: that life would freely flow over him, so that happiness, if it came, could find him open to it. I often see pictures of him in the newspapers. Always in the center, always smiling. And I hope he achieved it. Found moments of happiness, while success and money flowed over him.

I had become an established film star, with photographs and interviews in the press. I smiled from pictures taken in capitals most of my family only knew from the atlas. Smiling, arm in arm with famous and stupid and wise and kind and rich people.

Encountering situations I had never thought would come near me. Travels and impressions and kindness and goodness I hoped my subconscious would store up until misfortune came.

After a year, I went home on a visit. Walked past the theatre with a sense of true sorrow that I no longer belonged there. Sneaked into the auditorium during a rehearsal and sat in the darkness, reveling in the world I so much wanted to be part of. At the same time I felt a slight arrogance because I knew what I was now experiencing made up for the lines I was not speaking on that stage.

At home I spent hours in the kitchen, cooking the dishes I had composed in my imagination while eating restaurant dinners.

The sewing circle and friends—and the family.

Nearly everything was as it had been—yet at the same time we had all changed. Both in relation to each other and in the lives we lived.

I had stayed on an island, and I had traveled around in the

world. From my window I could see the trees and the blue-berries growing on land that was mine and feel the joy of ownership.

I felt a security in my mind. Watched Linn playing with other children and knew that she was happy.

I smiled.

When Linn was newly born I stood behind a tree and looked enviously at the nurse who marched by with my baby in a big blue baby carriage. I was afraid to offend her by asking if I could wheel the child myself. Especially as this was her first job and she had already been with me for two weeks when I finally gave birth.

Linn was fourteen days late and the whole time, morning and night, they kept calling me from the television station, where an entire crew was waiting for my baby to arrive so that they could start rehearsing a play I had rashly accepted to do months before.

The last few weeks I spent hiding guilt, afraid that every-one was angry with me.

When the child finally arrived, she was almost torn away from me by waiting grandmothers and relatives and nurses. I did not dare say that I would prefer to take care of her myself. Only at night was she mine alone.

Pet, my dog, watched Linn with sorrow. It lay under a sofa and only came out when reassured I would take it in my arms and scratch its stomach for as long as I had nursed the baby.

In my imagination the dog suffered so much that I felt I had to demonstrate my continued love for it by taking it for a walk alone while the nurse went out with Linn.

People who are afraid of hurting the feelings of a dachs-hund will sooner or later get into trouble, I thought, while the dog and I stood hidden behind a tree watching my first-born glide past.

It could have been the proudest day of my life.

I have spent hours completely involved in what I thought other people wished to see me doing. The fear of hurting, fear of authority, the need for love have put me in the most hopeless situations. I have suppressed my own desires and wishes and, ever eager to please, have done what I thought was expected of me.

I remember a castle in Sorrento, in which I found myself alone, encompassed by cold, damp stone walls. This was when I was living with Ingmar. The mayor had invited us to a local film festival and put this enormous mausoleum at our disposal.

As usual, I went a day ahead of him with all the luggage. I had to move into the castle all by myself. Ingmar never came. He stayed on his island writing a script, and said he had an ear inflammation. I had suspected that this would happen, but when I wanted to get a room in the hotel where the other festival participants were staying, I was dissuaded: as long as I stayed in the castle, officially Ingmar stayed there as well, or at least was on his way to do so. I was the sacrificial lamb offered up to avoid the scandal that their guest of honor had never turned up.

I, who as a child slept in the bathtub because that was the only place small enough to make me feel safe, now had a bedroom the size of a railway station. Below, on the first floor, were enormous silent spaces, endless corridors with armor and candelabra.

The bed stood in the middle of the floor, with me in it. I lay there and trembled, while I could hear the distant laughter and singing from the hotel.

I wanted to escape, but did not dare venture down those dark stairs. None of the doors would lock; the walls creaked and a grandfather clock struck every fifteen minutes.

I never thought I would survive the night, yet each morning I smiled to the festival officials and told them I had slept very well.

Fearful of not pleasing, fearful of hurting, fearful of destroying my disguise as a nice girl.

The last trip I had with my husband, Jappe, was to Poland. We arrived at a mountain resort, where some folk dancers were entertaining the guests. As the evening progressed, the audience began to join in, dancing in rhythm with the professionals, slapping their heels with their palms as they did. My husband laughed and was red in the face and kicked higher than anyone else. I sat safely in a corner, watching.

Bibi, who had come with us, called, "Now you must dance, Liv," and Jappe shouted, "Come on, dance!"

I drank vodka after vodka for courage, my palms sweaty with fear, knowing I was expected to embark on the floor.

I left the safety of my corner, let one of the dancers put an arm around my waist, and the next moment the music had swept him and me away. For a short time the room swirled round and round, and I giggled because it felt as if I was floating with it.

Far away I could hear my laughing husband say to Bibi: "Look at Liv! She's like an elephant dancing the polka."

The room stopped swirling. I saw all the faces turn toward me in laughter; and I tore myself free and ran out into the night. I ran and ran until I found a meadow where I could lie down in grass that was tall enough to hide me from the rest of the world. There I lay and nobody missed me; no one came to look for me.

After many hours I went up to bed.

A miserable elephant cried itself to sleep, feeling it could not go on living.

It is good to put behind one the desire to live the life of the surroundings. Get to know oneself better, understand the reason for one's needs. Perceive more clearly the motivations of others and recognize my own fear and insecurity in them.

THEY WERE FOUR CLEVER MEN AND THEY MOVED INTO my living room for a week with their cameras, lights, tape recorders and preconceived ideas.

I was famous and to be immortalized in a "personal portrait." I welcomed them and felt quite flattered. There was much I wanted to say, and I thought I'd come far enough to have the courage of my convictions.

When they left I stood on the steps waving goodbye, but inside I felt humiliated, a little stupid, and alone.

The living room was again my living room. I no longer needed to warn Linn to be careful of all the wires and tripods that for six days had been everywhere with strict instructions not to touch anything when the men left each evening for their hotel.

They never phoned to say thank you, and I wondered why I got the feeling that they had hurt me.

"We hope you will be very amusing," said the interviewer. He was preoccupied with his own private worries and mostly talked about loneliness. He wept when I told about mine. But the camera was not turned on him.

"This won't be interesting enough," said the producer, clasping his head in his hands when I talked.

The sound man borrowed my bed for an hour. He wasn't feeling well and had slept badly at the hotel—as they all did. Besides, they were longing for their own country.

The cameraman smiled to me at times as if to indicate he had never expected this all to turn out successfully, and that it was perfectly all right with him.

And I? Linn's nanny chose the first day of the interview to give notice. I had no idea how I was going to get another one. The man I lived with was hundreds of miles away and his life was full of problems, of which I seemed to be the greatest.

I wanted to explain to the interviewer that I really *could* laugh. But when his questions were so serious, his own voice so melancholy, and when he even had tears in his eyes most of the time, it was not easy for me to contribute humor.

Yet when they turned the camera on him and he repeated his questions he spoke lightly and easily and his eyes were all intelligence, without a trace of sorrow.

I had hoped for a dialogue, he wanted a monologue: my private thoughts and opinions. But what I said was to fit in with the picture he wished to present of me.

All four were very friendly and they went away, taking my face and voice on their rolls of film and tape, leaving an empty space in my house.

They let me express publicly a sorrow and a longing. They photographed my home and my child and my books—and thereby created an insecurity in me. Which they left behind.

HE TELLS HER THAT HER SOUL IS WIDE MOUNTAIN PLA-
teaus and then sudden deep dark abysses that he cannot look
into.

He has never understood her longing to lay her life open
for him.

The only abyss she is aware of in her soul is the one which
holds her fear and loneliness without him. And she weeps and
wishes he would set foot on the wide mountain plateaus.

He has a timetable to keep, a bad conscience he has to nurse
when he has been happy with her. He must go home to his
wife and children and dinner, and maybe find more pleasure
in them because she gave him the peace he needed.

And the woman of the wide mountain plateaus and the
deep abysses buys a book and goes home to her telephone.

His is the only hand she wants to hold and she wishes that
something could happen to make it possible and true for her
to find a new hand before she drowns.

But she also knows that when the day comes that finds her
with another, she will deliberately have to cut off the life in
her, embrace as if it were for the first time—in order to prove
through her poor faithful body that by being a part of another
man she has forgotten the one she loved.

And she knows that she will wake up afterward many,
many times, perhaps all her life, and long for him. Grieve
over that which used to be the two of them.

While she still has him, they go away to a warm country.
She holds his hand while he reads, and she feels a tranquillity
because everything is ordinary. She can afford the knowledge
that there are long periods when he doesn't think about her.
But she also knows that the hand resting in hers will soon give
it a quick hard squeeze to show that she exists for him.

Sometimes he turns and looks at her with happiness, and once in a great while there is uneasiness in the eyes. Then she knows he is thinking of his wife and children and she realizes with an icy clearness that he both loves her and is going to leave her.

As if he reads her thoughts, he puts away his book. "I can never live without you," he lies to her in the sun.

She believes him until he falls asleep, holding her close to him.

She knows when he wakes his sense of guilt will also awaken his need for security and order, his loyalty to what he feels is his responsibility. What he owes to another.

Beloved man.

I CAME TO HOLLYWOOD WITH A SUITCASE PACKED FOR TEN days. I had been invited to the premiere of *The Emigrants*. I remained for many months.

An astounded actress from Trondhjem was showered with offers. People smiled and said welcome, opened their homes, picked fruit from their trees and placed it in my child's hands.

I began working, and Linn and I moved into an enormous house with five bathrooms and a swimming pool and a guest cottage; wrote letters to friends saying that people here must be crazy, but it was fun. My bathroom was the size of an ordinary Oslo apartment. It was so grand that the toilet was built like a throne so that one should never feel confused being a film star when nature called.

"You must cut your hair," said one producer.

"No!"

"I'll make you the biggest star if you'll just dress a little differently."

"I'm used to dressing this way."

"Perhaps you should wear some more make-up. Send the beauty-parlor bill to me."

"Certainly not."

And then they left me alone. After all, I enjoyed the status of a serious actress. I had soul and depth, and was European. I didn't use make-up, and I came from Norway.

I met with generosity, found friends and acquaintances, bathed in heated swimming pools, sat in soft chairs watching films in private screening rooms, walked on long sandy beaches by the sea.

I stood on my lawn in the morning squinting up at the sun, was driven to the studio before most people were awake—at half-past five, when the best of day and night meet.

As I sat in his chair, the make-up artist and I gossiped. He gave me good advice for my new life and was always around, as if he wanted to make sure that I didn't get into difficulties. For many years, even before I was born, he had been bending over world-famous faces, covering them with creams and rouges and powders. The bodies of women who had been the cause of sweet dreams for men all over the world had relaxed here in loose dressing gowns, enjoying a moment of freedom before being taken to the wardrobe and laced in and padded out in the appropriate places.

"Life is so short," said the make-up artist, "and no one can persuade me to give something up today for the possibilities of tomorrow, promises of the future." His neck and hands were covered with chains and amulets, and he jingled gaily as he moved. He wore a little cap to hide his baldness.

"Sparkle," he whispered to me as I went in to the lights and the heat and the cameras. "That's what Shirley Temple's mother always said to her little daughter."

I spent some months in Hollywood and tried to sparkle. When something inside me protested, I reminded myself I would soon be home again. I was looking forward to making a film on the island in Sweden, living with old friends in primitive summer cottages where there was no hot water or electricity. Walk a hundred yards to an outhouse, whatever the weather.

Sit there and see the sea through the cracks in the wall, and feel that it is good to be alive.

When your profession takes you one day to Hollywood and the next to a barren island in the Baltic.

IT BECAME MORE DIFFICULT TO WALK IN THE STREETS without being recognized. Strangers would come up to me and say, "Excuse me. Aren't you Liv Ullmann?" The old bashfulness returned, making me as confused as ever, only now it was mixed with other, more complicated emotions. I replied to compliments by listening with a smile, listened and then moved away, partly to stop myself from being seduced by the flattery.

I had not accomplished anything fantastic in myself, but I had experienced and understood something. At times my conscience no longer bothered me because of all that I did not do and did not know. I found pleasure in my new-found ability to make my own decisions (even when they were bad), took delight in my work, in being angry, in weeping, in laughing, in living.

Joy in allowing myself to be me, positive or negative.

It wasn't any miracle that had changed me. I didn't live happily ever afterward. I was often afraid.

But I was richer within; I was better friends with myself.

The difficulty was the struggle against everything around me: certain books, television programs, films, newspapers— the mass media shouting every day what a happy person should consist of, promising the gigantic, the triumphant.

And there I sat with my little, simple happiness, satisfied with what I had, until it was pointed out to me that love, for example, so beautifully sung and written and painted, was much more than what I had.

I was afraid at times and woke up and cried out in the night, because whatever I arrived at—every time I thought I had reached something—they exclaimed that there was something better to be had.

But I was fighting all the time to be able to rest in what was mine, to enjoy the warmest and best feeling of the moment, and not all the time be thinking, Oh, God, this isn't enough.

Many of my dreams were never to be fulfilled, but I had found what I had never dreamed of: reality can be magnificent even when life is not.

My hands began to shake; sometimes I had to hold a glass with both hands. I used to be able to sleep anywhere at any time, but now I often lay awake.

I caught myself passing by a genuine situation without stopping and becoming part of it, and then reproducing the same reality on screen with all my compassion.

When I encountered a drunk man in the street, I followed him—not to help, but to study the way he set his feet down, how his arms hung limp and dangled at his sides.

Other people were objects I could meet and use for professional purposes.

I wiped the tears from the eyes of a character I was playing and walked blindly past tears in my home.

Oh, yes. I saw the dangers. Hesitated.

I met an athlete who had reached the top. Heard him talking of his record race when there were tenths of a second between him and the next man. What had he sacrificed for those moments? What did the reverse side of his medal look like? Had he not paid for his few seconds of triumph with days and months and years during which he had had to say no to everything else?

Was this what I was using my new-won freedom for?

I packed my bags and went home to Oslo, signed a contract with the Norwegian Theatre. At last I had a professional link with Norway again.

I was like a figurehead on an old ship. She who is standing seemingly so proudly at the bow and plows through the waves and gazes ahead, while her whole body, at an angle, is pressed close to the ship to which she belongs.

ONE THING I LEARNED:

That a husband is a sort of alibi for a woman. Never mind what it looks like behind the scenes.

He may be fat and stupid and old, but nonetheless he can condemn the woman's flabby body and menopause, and encounter only sympathy if he exchanges her for a younger one. This goes for professional life. This goes for private life.

I have had periods of living in the exposed position a single or divorced woman has to cope with. Been the woman who everyone knows "doesn't have someone."

A man can go to a restaurant alone in the evening; I cannot, without letting myself be: (*a*) criticized, (*b*) offered male company I am not interested in, (*c*) pitied.

In discussing my salary, I have asked for the same as a male colleague. Though we have been with the theatre the same number of years, I am told that he must have more than me because he supports a family. I, who have a child and a home and responsibilities, am not in this category. Because I am a woman.

I am the breadwinner of my family, but I don't have free help in my house in the guise of a wife, as he has.

In divorce proceedings, the husband more often has a choice.

The woman is made to feel guilty if she wants or needs to work and let others look after her child. Because she is a woman the child needs her at home. Because he is a man, it is normal that he gives prior attention to his profession.

When the man and the woman don't marry, she is the mother with an illegitimate child.

She has the responsibility. She has to arrange eighteen years of her life in accordance with what is best for the child. She has to refuse work and contact with other people when she cannot afford or get help. She has to run home and be on time because she knows whoever is helping her will leave if she feels she is being exploited.

I look at my allowance and wonder what women do who cannot provide for their children themselves, but have to depend on what a man considers a reasonable maintenance.

I have girlfriends who have not left the house in the evening for a whole year, because they are exhausted by their double responsibility: the rush to keep the timetable, the bad conscience, lack of sleep. They suppress their need for emotional contact with others than their child until sometime in the future, when they will be able to *sleep,* rest, have a day that is their own.

But, fortunately, the lone mother gets the kisses, the notes on her pillow, the confidences, the bodily warmth, the responsibility. Is close to the child every day. Emotionally she has an endless advantage over the man.

I have stopped accepting invitations where women are only seen as an appendage of a man, and I am nothing because I am single. But I no longer let it irritate me; those gatherings where my sex is not equal in value to a man's are gatherings I can do without.

To be a woman is to have the same needs and longings as a man.

We need love and we wish to give it.

If only we all could accept that there is no difference between us where human values are concerned. Whatever sex. Whatever the life we have chosen to live.

I have my periods and my menopause; and my horror of sagging breasts, and my awareness of the young girl who is me and whom you can no longer see in my face.

And *he* has his prestige and difficulties in his job and his fear of going bald and becoming impotent and his doubts; and the insecurity he has from when he was thirteen.

We are together with our problems. We are not dangerous or threatening to each other—not in the moment we feel that we *need* each other.

AT THE END OF 1972 AN AMERICAN FILM MAGAZINE printed a long article about me, and on the cover under my smiling face you could read: "THE STORY OF A WINNER."

Here is a week chosen at random from that time:

A DIARY OF A WINNER

Monday

The most incredible things can happen in Hollywood. One can become a star overnight. Jewels and furs can suddenly appear on the doormat. But I think only I have *nine* Christmas trees.

One of them is for Linn, but she is going home to her grandmother and cousins and a white Christmas in Norway.

Friends are sitting on the floor in my hotel corridor decorating a tree that will be waiting for me when I get back from taking Linn to the airport. They have bought colored balls and long strings of Swedish flags—but that is not an uncommon mistake in Hollywood, where Norway is thought to be some province in Scandinavia.

My friends are waiting by my door when I return and I take their lovely present into the room, which they had envisioned empty and desolate after my daughter's departure.

They gasp with admiration, because along the walls and in the corners there are Christmas trees of every shape and color glistening and shining with big and little magical lights. One of them even rotates and sings carols.

The famous Movie Hero fetches me for dinner. He brings an enormous fir tree covered with artificial silver and imitation pearls. Unfortunately, he resembles my first love and when anyone does that, red warning lights switch on inside me. It is very difficult in America when those lights start blinking—because American men say "I love you" as part of the conversation.

And when the man is one of the Famous you cannot laugh it off; because they have such sensitive egos, and think they never give better performances than when they half-close their velvet eyes over a glass of wine and whisper lines from the films in which they have acted.

The next day all the papers proclaim that the famous Movie Hero and I are lovers.

Tuesday

I am invited to dinner at Hugh Hefner's, publisher of *Playboy*. Upon our arrival we have to pass through several electric gates with built-in television cameras. Pictures of all who pass through are flashed onto a screen in the guardhouse, scrutinized by three private detectives with loaded revolvers in their belts. There have been several attempted burglaries and crimes of violence. Only a few weeks previously in this same neighborhood bestial murders were committed without any other purpose or motive than the murderer's delight in killing those who, in his eyes, were too rich and successful.

The Playboy king is wearing terry-cloth pajamas. Some girls walk about with long furry rabbits' ears fastened to their heads and little round tails on their bottoms.

We look at films: A dog makes love to a girl. I think of Pet and hope she will not discover what I am doing.

Afterward we sit in small groups, not knowing what to talk about because our host is asleep on the sofa and the rest of us don't know each other that well. The rabbit girls show some of the guests around the house.

I walk through the grounds. An artificial mountain in the garden. Inside it a subterranean grotto with swirling warmed waves. Two people are doing things in the water under red and blue spotlights.

Wednesday

A long working day. In the early morning, dress rehearsal for *40 Carats*, after an endless drive with a chauffeur who used to play cowboy roles and does not realize that he keeps clicking the false teeth in his mouth all the time.

Later there is skating practice. Ten men, headed by the director, the photographer and the producer, follow me to see what I can do. Even though in the film I am meant to appear clumsy and out of practice (just as a woman of forty is believed to be), they now want to see if I can stay on my feet at all.

I haven't skated since I was a child. Memories of fiascos on cold skating rinks in Trondhjem when I was awkward and thirteen years old, with wobbly knees and ankles that buckled. Evening after evening, hoping to learn the art—so that one day I could glide through the soft darkness accompanied by caressing music, hand in hand with James Stewart.

Now, years later, the only difference is the applause from my ten attendants. Then they ask if I would like a stand-in.

Lunch. A Swedish journalist sits waiting for me on the lawn outside the canteen. Not having read this week's papers, he thinks I am still going with last week's Film Hero. Fifteen minutes of the precious lunch break are spent on him, so the papers at home will not report that I have become "stuck up."

In the dining room wait an agent and a producer. They want to consult with me about who is to have the male lead in my next film. I am delighted at being asked, even though I know that it is all a pretense laid on to please me. I suspect that somewhere is an actor with a signed contract being consulted in the same way about me.

In the afternoon I try on hats. The same crowd as in the morning gathers in the producer's office to learn from me how far down over my forehead I want the brims. *I*, who am so unsure about taste in clothes that I will change a dress if my daughter sends me a critical look.

Then an interview: "You were so sad in that article in the *Los Angeles Times*," they tell me. "Could you give us an amusing version?"

I have just been through the opening of my first Hollywood film, which no one liked.

"You were wonderful," they say, and embrace me.

In the evening I attend a ball. The most famous of the guests are placed on a stage, where they are to eat. There we sit in tiers, one above the other, turned toward the hall so that those who have paid for their food can watch us chew ours and see that we chat and behave like ordinary, simple people.

Mae West is borne in between two strong men with long hair and open-necked shirts with masses of muscles underneath. They whisper in my ear that these are her lovers. She has yellow corkscrew curls and her face is heavily made up, and she has false eyelashes that are coming loose. They ask me to come and meet her. She so wants to know me. Dumbly we grasp each other's hands.

As I walk away, I hear her hiss to one of the lovers, "Who the hell was that?"

Thursday
Call Linn in Norway. She says she is busy watching television, so could I please be brief. I tell her about the tree she

has been given. It is big; the branches are caramel and choco-late, the trunk made of candies in every color, and the whole tree is covered with little lights that twinkle and twinkle and twinkle.

Later in the day I fly to New York. The trip lasts five and a half hours and I sleep the whole way. That is what I love about flying: there are no telephone calls. It is like a gift of time—time that I have all to myself.

At the airport, there are photographers, cars, and people I ought to recognize. At the hotel I have been given the best suite, overloaded with flowers and fruit. I long for all the people I don't recognize to leave my room! Who are they? What do they want? And why?

I stand looking out at New York from the thirtieth floor. Enormous buildings for human beings, almost touching the sky. The cars below so closely packed you cannot see the street.

Then I walk through the enormous spaces that are my rooms, my home for a few days. On the wall is posted a list telling me what to do if I want a pleasant stay: never be in the room without putting the chain on the door; never let anyone in who says he has come to repair the television; never speak to strangers in the lobby.

A sudden memory of Linn. Linn at a grownups' party the day before she left: all the guests have been given musical instruments. And we sit on the floor and sing and play our instruments and laugh.

Linn asks if she may sing a solo, and we are all silent for her. Very serious, she sings "London Bridge Is Falling Down."

Somewhere inside me an old dream awakens—a vision: the rightness of having several generations gathered in mutual pleasure in the same room, enjoying each other.

Linn later that evening: I see her through the veranda window. She is sitting on a sofa with an old man. Her head is moving. I see only their backs and her gesticulating hands. She is living her own life out there.

For a few years still, she will be the center of her own universe, as *I* once was in mine—until she was born and I experienced it as a gift to see *her* take my place in me.

Friday

Formal lunch with *Time* magazine. The senior executives have invited me to meet with them in their most private dining room. They want to do a cover story about me and I am to be examined to find out if I am enough of a personality for such an honor. During a barrage of questions and provocations across the large round table, I try to eat something as well. I still have a long day's work ahead of me. *They* are tough men, but *I* am a woman from Trondhjem.

For the last two weeks a reporter from *Time* has been with me while I filmed in Greece, and then on the plane to Los Angeles for endless hours—so that I didn't dare go to sleep in case my mouth fell open. Some secrets must be kept from the press. We became good friends and parted like brother and sister after a week in Hollywood.

Now I am told that another writer is to be with me in New York. Over the coffee I ask the new one why he has suddenly appeared on the scene. He tells me it is because he is tough and level-headed and not easily fooled. *Time* wants to counterbalance the positive information it has gathered, and is now looking for the negative side of Miss Ullmann.

And he is there to reveal it.

I willingly share with him my weaknesses, ladle out how bad I really am, yet in a way that I hope will charm the boots off him.

By evening I am dead tired and longing for home. On my bedside table is a kind of tree I always have with me. It is a little twisted plant, and on its branches hang various brass objects, each with its own significance. I imagine it brings me luck. It was given to me by a great actress when I left the National Theatre and set forth into the world.

I telephone to say I am unable to keep a dinner appointment. Give instructions for no calls to be put through. Pull the blankets over my head. Wake up in the middle of the night with troubling thoughts provoked by the *Time* interview.

Saturday

Filming in the streets of New York. Wearing tailor-made suits and smart hats in the middle of the world's largest city. People gathering to look. Cars and skyscrapers and faces merging. Autograph hunters moving about in a clump, glued together by their common interest.

Hairdresser, make-up man, dresser—the three are never more than a few steps away. They adjust me: pluck at my hair, dab at my face, pull at my clothes, showing their friendliness; and all the while I must maintain my concentration. Smile and be friendly back.

I think of the time when Mamma, Bitten and I were here some years ago. We wanted to have a drink in the Plaza Hotel, but were not allowed in because we were wearing slacks. Mamma indignantly explaining in agitated Trondhjem English that she was out with her daughters and such treatment was insolent. It could never have happened in the America *she* lived in thirty years before.

Now, in the afternoon, I am here again, am filming in the heart of the Plaza Hotel, working in its elegant red and golden vestibule.

There are so many people wanting to watch that they look like a great chorus lining the walls.

Television, radio and journalists.

A fat, officious woman asks who the star is.

"Liv Ullmann," I say modestly.

"I don't know her. It can't be a good film."

When we have finished for the day, I meet the journalist from *Time*. He gives me a copy of his book about Vietnam—he was a correspondent there for a year. I like him. We talk about war and pollution, about children and love, discover a quick, spontaneous agreement that colors our conversations, turns our meeting into a feast of thoughts and ideas.

At least this is how I experience it.

He may write about me as nastily as he likes; at least we *talked* together.

In the evening Max von Sydow visits me. He is one of my best working companions and a close friend as well, ever since *Hour of the Wolf,* the film where we met, when I was very pregnant with Linn.

We have a picnic on the floor of my suite. Potted plants we transform into trees, and the silk cushions are grass and flowers.

The Plaza Hotel is so elegant that the waiter's expression never changes: just a slight quiver of the nostrils when he goes down on his knees and serves us dinner on the wall-to-wall carpet.

Sunday

Back in Los Angeles. Christmas. Christmas trees in all the streets. Lights in the windows and colorful decorations on the doors. So different from Norway:

The white silence in the woods. The snow and the spruce and the tracks of skis.

Here the sun is shining and I go out in a thin jacket. I cannot stand being in the hotel room with all the Christmas trees glinting at me.

Seven o'clock on Christmas Eve and I am on my way back from the studio. At home everyone will be sitting eating spare ribs and sauerkraut.

Four young girls—very young—in a window we drive past. They are happy, they lean out, laugh to the cars and the people in them. They are slim, have tousled hair.

A stab in the heart of yearning and fear because those days will never come again.

I bring two of my Christmas trees into my bedroom.

One is from Linn. She has decorated it with angels and Santas she made herself.

The other is from a close friend. It is stuck in a pot of earth.

"So that you can plant it in America when you leave," he says, "then you will have a root here as well."

LINN IS BACK AND WE ARE ON THE BEACH IN MALIBU, frying mussels and drinking wine. Everything is white: the houses, the sand, the wine; even the quivering air is of a clear light substance. Linn is given a present of four incredible frogs that have to be fed live grasshoppers twice a month. She cries when I say we cannot keep them.

We make a big bonfire on the beach, even though it is the middle of the day.

Someone plays a guitar and sings. Linn dances for us.

Together with Linn, I pretend I am little again and I run with her along the water's edge laughing at the waves; inspect the shells that are washed ashore; peer at flowers we do not have in Norway.

She finds a bird that has been hurt and holds it in her hands until she thinks its heart is not pounding with terror anymore. Then, when one of the grownups suggests that it would be best to kill it because it is wounded, she goes and hides.

She is the only child, but we all play the same games. Nothing stops her, and she dashes off, a tanned little body with flaxen hair atop, behind her a laughing group of adults forming a long tail.

Later there is a big dinner in Beverly Hills. My producer is giving a party for me. We all drive there in a bus. The limousine sent by the studio follows. We laugh at this and say to each other we are traveling in style.

Paul Kohner, my American agent, makes a speech, addressing a coming big star at the table. I believe it is me until I see Linn wriggling in her chair, tugging at her hair and smiling with eyes closed. And she is right (she almost always is); it is she!

He raises his glass to the child, and the hundred guests, whom we scarcely know, get to their feet and smile at her—the way they know how to do it in Hollywood. She loves it, while she hides her head in my lap. I reflect that it is a good thing we are going home soon to Norway.

Later we are shown a film. She and I sit together in the dark. This is the first time she has been in a cinema. She is five. I can just see her face in the light from the screen. Quick, whispered questions, sudden apprehension, and then delight—a little mouth moving in wordless attention. All is real. Here and now. Her hand in mine. Our closeness in experiencing something together.

The drive home. Thin little fingers entwined in mine.

The hotel room is large and in semidarkness. We sit beside the window, looking out into the night. After a while we draw the heavy curtains and I order up a large glass of milk. She is allowed to sit in her pajamas drinking it in front of the television.

I tell her that when *I* was little we didn't have television. She looks at me with pity and I become old right before her eyes. She asks if we drove about in a horse and buggy in the old days. When I was a girl.

She drinks her milk in careful sips, so as to prolong the day as much as possible.

It is late night. A little child falls asleep in a chair. Carefully I carry her to a big, broad bed, where the sheets are changed every day, and the mattress is soft and generous.

In the distance I can hear the cars whizzing past on Sunset Boulevard, and the sounds of night life.

I AM EXPECTING AN IMPORTANT VISITOR.

Henry Kissinger is to escort me to a big ball.

He has inquired in Los Angeles who would be the most suitable date for him on this "event of the year" in Hollywood. Someone came up with me, and for a couple of days they have been calling me from the White House. Today he called himself.

It is the year of his glory, and everybody wants to meet him. Later it turns out to be two days before the whole Watergate story will begin to put an end to the President. This will be Nixon's last public appearance before the scandal is known by the whole world.

Everybody seems to want to share with me the meeting with Kissinger. I have piled cushions and blankets on top of the telephone, in order not to hear.

A girlfriend from home is to pose as my private secretary. Impatiently we lean out of the window, trying to guess which of the cars lining up in front of the hotel is his.

"Perhaps he is so modest he drives that little red one," my friend suggests.

I look at her indulgently. Safety precautions in political life cannot be fitted into a Volkswagen.

Since Mr. Kissinger is the first blind date of my life, I was confused on the telephone and forgot to ask when he would fetch me. Consequently both the "secretary" and I have been dressed up for the last three hours.

From some official department in Norway has come a letter about oil. It is obvious they want me to inform Mr. Kissinger about something, but it's not clear to me what. (It turns out he didn't even know we had found oil.)

From Sweden I receive a note from the secretary of a certain politician asking me to deny some comments he has made about Kissinger. (A week later he repeats his comments at a press conference.)

Anonymous threatening letters lie crumpled up in the wastepaper basket. (I think of them sometimes when I wake up in the night.)

The telephone growls underneath its covers.

I know what his favorite wine is. It has been standing in ice that melted several hours ago.

My suite has been searched—so whoever recommended me was not convincing enough: I might still be a secret agent or have bombs under my bed.

All this is very unusual for someone who never had a blind date, and I become so agitated that I change my dress, and choose one that is less pretty than the one I was wearing originally.

A Norwegian journalist sends up his card, asking if he may disguise himself as a butler. He has come all the way from Oslo hoping for this. We reply that the post is already filled.

The "secretary" and I go through the program again: how she is to serve the wine, perhaps mention something about oil in a passing remark, bumble about a little, tidy up some papers—and then keep quiet.

A knock at the door.

We both make a rush for it, stumbling over each other. I give her a push and snarl that plans have changed. I shall open the door myself.

He is smiling and much smaller than I. I know I picked the wrong shoes.

We shake hands while he waves reassuringly to some grave-faced men in the corridor.

She who is to pour wine lets most of it spill on his trousers. Feverishly all three of us try to remove the stain, and in the end one can hardly see it.

It is only in the elevator that I realize that the cleaner's tag is still attached to my second-best dress, and I tug and tug and tug, and tug off a little bit of the dress as well. The strap has gone on my handbag.

The "secretary" remarks on my return that this was clearly visible on television.

I swish into a car with bulletproof windows, followed by men with little microphones into which they speak all the time.

I think that I am very far from Trondhjem.

Late at night, I lie in the double bed with my girlfriend the "secretary," who has stayed awake waiting for my report.

I have a thousand things to tell her—and then the telephone rings. It is the Norwegian journalist, talking from the lobby. His trip has cost hundreds of dollars, he has waited all night, he reminds me of a service he once did me. After a long discussion and a few threats, he works himself up to my bedside. Notebook in hand, he looks at me expectantly and asks me to tell him what I said to Kissinger and, more important, what Kissinger told me. I am silent, but my friend mutters something about a light she thought she saw around his head. In my heart I forgive her, because she has been up alone all evening waiting to express herself. Besides, she must be quite tired now.

The next day I am waltzing through the world press, saying: "It is as though there is a halo over Henry Kissinger."

THE SEWING CIRCLE IS VISITING HOLLYWOOD.

When one of its members has been nominated for an Oscar, it is only proper that the girls gather.

The Heroine is convinced that there will be no prize for her.

The hotel room gradually fills with people, who all assure her they have heard—they know—there is no doubt: She is going to win!

In the end she almost believes it herself. Her cheeks acquire a hectic flush and when her friends send her to bed so that she can be beautiful in the evening, she is quite unable to rest.

The Mother has also come to Hollywood. Now she sits in her room and wishes that all will go well for the Baby.

The sewing circle answers telephone calls fom east and west; sorts out the telegrams of congratulations which are sent in advance, just in case; arranges the bouquets; and dashes to the windows and looks down on the palm trees and the people. Finally switches on the television, where everyone is talking about the Oscar awards.

The girlfriends, too, become flushed and wake the Heroine, who pretends to be asleep.

All four sit on the broad bed and open a bottle of champagne, send for Russian caviar, and say to each other that people at home should see them now.

Then come the hairdresser and the make-up artist, good friends from several films in America. Both have insisted they be allowed to fix her up a little.

They, too, have champagne, but don't become as ruffled as the sewing circle. Many Oscar candidates have passed through their hands. Kind and efficient, they cover her nervousness with make-up and curls. When they finish, she is hardly recognizable. The girlfriends fetch the new dress, and for a moment the Heroine feels like the Ugly Duckling at its first meeting with the swans.

The Mother sits on a sofa and has tears in her eyes when the Baby is presented in her final version. She feels this is the most suitable reaction for a mother under such circumstances.

The Agent arrives. Smiling and friendly, bearing presents for everyone.

He has never before been visited by a sewing circle from Norway.

The Heroine sees that for the first time he, too, has nerves. He is a little too eager to assure them that this is not the end of the world. If she does not get an Oscar this year, she will another time.

Everyone assures everyone else that of course it doesn't make any difference whether she wins or not. But in their thoughts they are planning where in her living room they will place the award.

The car is waiting for them at the entrance. Long and black, as usual. The chauffeur does not seem aware of the gravity of the occasion. His eyes are tired. He hates Oscar nights because all the streets are jammed. Long black ships glide through the night, laden with people in their grand costumes. Made-up faces glance solemnly at other passing cargoes.

They are there!

A confusion of spotlights and police and guards and photographers. Enormous scaffolds have been erected. People are packed together as at a football stadium. Names are called over loudspeakers. Flashbulbs explode.

The Heroine from Trondhjem is trembling all over. She cannot smile, because her mouth no longer obeys her.

She is led up onto platforms and is interviewed for television and introduced over loudspeakers and applauded and appraised while she passes the football crowd.

Here and there she hears a greeting in her own language and feels a rush of gratitude as she stumbles along the red carpet.

She would like to explain to those who look friendly why she cannot smile back.

The sewing circle, watching it all on television at the hotel, is in a state of agitation and phones relatives in Norway to say the suspense is unbearable.

The Heroine is taken to an enormous hall and seated in the same row as the other candidates. They glance searchingly at each other, smile, and wish each other good fortune. They all look more beautiful and more assured than she does, reflects the Heroine sadly.

Of all those present, the Mother is the only one who thinks that no one equals the Baby, and that if they cannot see that, so much the worse for them. And then she cries a bit into her handkerchief again.

The hall is packed with expectancy and fear and investments. On the stage a glittering show broadcast all over America and many other places in the world.

Name after name is called out. Every branch of the film industry is to be rewarded. Only near the end the camera turns on five pale women's faces. The sewing circle remarks that she looks quite calm and notes that it must tell her.

The Heroine is just then wondering about one of the other nominees, who has gone out and changed her dress in the middle of the proceedings. She feels it must make an eventual disappointment all the greater if you dress up for victory in advance.

The winner's name is called—and it is neither the Heroine

nor the Confident. She sees tears come to the other's eyes—a despairing star who collapses against someone's shoulder. Suddenly, the Heroine understands that much more has been at stake here than what she herself is going through. Slowly she is filled with a wonderful sense of relief, while she applauds the winner on the stage.

The sewing circle remarks on how well she takes it. Look how she smiles.

For the first time that day it is possible to control the mouth. And she gets up when it's all over, laughs toward the Agent and pats the Mother's cheek and watches the Confident depart in dark glasses.

She tries to ignore the fact that she now has a new part, mirrored in everyone's consoling thump on her back: the Loser.

Outside are hundreds of autograph-hunters and they hurl themselves at her, still remembering her from television.

She has written her name a few times, when she hears a screech as from a thousand gulls.

And there comes the Winner.

The autograph books are torn from her, the name half-written on a paper she is holding. She is almost trampled underfoot as they rush past her in their pursuit of the Successful One.

When the Heroine gets back to the hotel after a long night, there is a note on her pillow:

"We think you were the best. Wake us when you come home. Regards from the sewing circle."

Again the mouth smiles. Now it is as if it can't stop smiling.

JAN TROELL WAS SECURE IN HIS OWN COUNTRY. HE PADDED about with a camera, captured the most beautiful landscapes, photographing for posterity life between people in a way few could emulate.

The Emigrants and *The New Land* were great successes in Scandinavia, first as films and later on television. And when they were shown in America, the films were praised and celebrated there as well.

Now Jan and I met again, after working together in Sweden; this time in California, to make *Zandy's Bride* for Warner Brothers.

He was homesick the whole time.

Where previously he had been surrounded by a team of fifteen, who worked together for a year of warmth and trust and friendship, he now met with a hundred total strangers.

We filmed in the lovely mountains near Carmel, one of the most wonderful landscapes in America: Big Sur.

Every morning we drove in long black limousines from the hotel with its heated swimming pool and hamburgers. We would leave in thick mist, stare into the gray and tell each other that there could not possibly be enough light for filming today. After an hour the cars left the highway to continue on a narrow, twisted road. Another hour of winding up the mountain, still in mist. Then all at once—in the space of a few feet—just around a bend—the landscape opened in all its glory. We came to a new nature and a different climate. Under us the fog. Here, far up, we found the same miracle day after day: a world of blazing sun and enormous green slopes, meadow flowers I had never seen before. There were wild pigs and mountain lions and many, many rattlesnakes.

They had built a little homestead, complete in every detail, painted and made to look as if it had been there, half over-shadowed by enormous elms, for an eternity of years.

There they waited every morning for Jan: the crew of a hundred.

Seeing them always gave him a shock, and he would take Gene Hackman and me aside, trying to make the intimate moment with us last as long as possible. Until, with dragging feet, he had to walk to the others; issue instructions, plan, be the leader—everything that he didn't want and couldn't do. While he looked with longing at the camera, his instrument, which he was not allowed to touch here. The union kept a sharp watch to ensure that everyone kept to his own job; and in America, Jan's contract only gave him permission to direct.

Once we shut ourselves inside the little house and said that we wanted to rehearse on our own. Jan had a hand-held camera. It was almost like the old days. Following my move-ments as if he were a part of me, sensitively and closely he photographed one of the loveliest scenes in the film: when Hanna is yearning to get away, looks at her few belongings from home, and collapses in tears over her traveling chest.

They invited this great artist to their country because they admired the poetry conveyed in his pictures. Then they took his tool from his hands and hoped he would repeat the miracle for them.

I, who didn't have his responsibility, was happy. Nature was the basis of this joy. I had forgotten that field flowers looked like this. How good it was to sit on the ground and feel the freshness of pure air all around me.

I broke out in a rash all over my body from poisonous plants that grew there, stepped cautiously so as not to surprise a snake in the grass. Enjoyed the sight of Linn when she rode about with the men who looked after the horses.

Under a tree Jan Troell sat and wrote letters home.

I HAVE READ ABOUT HIM IN FILM MAGAZINES. SIGHED OVER his blue eyes at the movies. Thought that only a good person could have such a lovely smile.

Oh, treacherous screen!

We have been invited to his big house in Beverly Hills. My Swedish nursemaid, Gunvor, who grew up on a small farm in Norrland but has become blasé here, sinks down into a deep sofa and announces that such houses give her a headache. She is twenty and indispensable to Linn and me.

"I must ask you to put your daughter in a bathing suit," he says. His three-year-old son is there on a visit. "His mother will be very unhappy if she hears he has been swimming with a nude girl at my home."

Gunvor exhales despairingly into the air, her whole body an expression of loathing for film stars, swimming pools, and this particular little boy.

When lunchtime comes, he tells her she is to eat in the kitchen. I look at him, am shocked, because it is obvious he is not joking.

At the table he lectures Linn, until she cries, that children don't talk while they eat. Only his two eldest are allowed to take part in a conversation which he supervises. I am numb.

The radio announces that I have received an award as the year's best actress. He hastens to tell me how little that means. The best films and actors are by-passed on political grounds. In passing, he tells me that it was very silly of me to have allowed that cover story in *Time*.

"It's death for an actor."

He himself has fought for years to keep them at arm's length.

And then we laugh loudly and heartily at my having been

so stupid. We laugh until Gunvor puts her head around the kitchen door and rolls her eyes to heaven.

She is allowed to join us for coffee, because then one of his old films is being shown on TV.

Afterward we discuss in detail the scenes he likes best. Until Gunvor, with a devil in her eyes, starts talking about my award. His face becomes pale and he stands up in the middle of something she is saying to announce that he has work to do, and must drive us home now.

He drops us outside the hotel, and the devils in Gunvor's eyes have now been replaced by angels, and she takes his hand and curtsies, and says thank you for the chance to be close to him and promises that she will tell all her girlfriends in Sweden that she has met him *in person*.

He tells me I have a sweet nanny.

Linn and Gunvor and I celebrate our dismissal with cocoa and cream in Linn's bed.

LINN AND I GO FOR A WALK IN BEVERLY HILLS.

We are the only ones who stroll in these streets.

There is a smell of rain-drenched lawns and flowers. Bushes ripe with all the colors of the world.

We talk about life—about men and women and children, about griefs and happiness we know and about strange dreams we have when asleep.

Linn knows much more than I. She has a built-in wisdom that I never knew.

We talk about responsibility, and she tells me that in fact she doesn't need me:

"You only decide two things for me: that I'm to fetch the newspaper in the morning and at what time I must go to bed. And you look after me and give me food. That's all."

At this moment Linn and I are close. Walking on a street far from home talking about friends in Norway. About her father and the strawberries that at this very moment perhaps cover the ground on his island.

"What is life, Mamma?" Linn asks. "Is it just people?"

She looks at some tiny insects crawling along the ground by our feet.

I tell her that when I was a child, there were surely more kinds of crawling things, but people destroyed their possibilities for life, in the same way we have destroyed birds and plants and animals. Creatures she will never see. And we who remember them will not live long enough to keep the memory of them alive.

"The world of flowers and play and dreams and belief which is still yours, Linn," I say, "the one you share with me at this moment—that world you will forget. Even if life itself— what no one can teach you—lives in you now."

Linn will grow up into a world where one has never seen anything but seas and air that are impoverished. Where stars *I* saw, when I was small, cannot be seen any longer.

She, who can switch on television when she wants company, who will cram in dates and grammar, and be surrounded by indigestible information from the society she lives in—she who is so alive and free today—will slowly be ground in the mill out of which only adults come.

We sit down in a patch of shade from a palm tree and I tell her about an orchid I once heard about. It can live in the heat of Africa or the ice of Greenland. And the strangest thing is, I tell my girl, that it can retain its fertile seed within itself for several hundred years. So that the two of us one day might find it and plant it in our garden, and with care bring forth life that had its beginning such a long time ago.

I tell her about a special flower that grows in France and has taken the shape and fragrance desired by a bee that lives only there.

Maybe it is like this because thousands of years' experience let it know whom to seduce and how. But one can also choose to believe that it was God who gave the flower this gift.

Linn listens with an open mouth. Reality, such as I know it, is suddenly close to the world of fantasy that is hers.

We watch a dog run past, followed by a fat, out-of-breath woman. We sense a thought in a glance it gives us. A bird hops about and cocks its head and wonders at two people so quiet here where almost everything else is some kind of bustle.

IT IS THE DAY BEFORE TWO GREAT POWERS ARE TO SIGN AN important pact.

Nixon and Brezhnev meet at a dinner in the Russian embassy.

I sit between the Russian ambassador and Kissinger.

Surprised by what is happening around me, I try to interpret codes in the buzz of clichés across the table. I am in the middle of a sacred male fraternity and after a while feel as I did at school when the boys were discussing something and I found it difficult to believe that they really were serious with their important looks and formulations.

Gromyko is pale and sits hunched at a corner of the table, with a mouth that is tight-pressed and sad.

He reminds me of a melancholy uncle who came to my wedding.

But I see humor in his eyes, too. Every time his name is mentioned in a speech he blushes.

Brezhnev looks a little vain, but I feel an immediate liking for him when he takes my hand between his two broad palms and tells me that he loved *The Emigrants*. I thank God I am devoid of any political influence, seeing that I fall so easily for flattery. Seated, Nixon looks so tiny. His torso is almost smaller than his head. The make-up has melted slightly and I am glad for his sake that the picture-taking is over. I feel a sort of compassion for this face. Where the black around the eyes has smeared a bit. He would have made a fantastic tragic figure in a Bergman film, if only he were a better actor.

We eat flown-in caviar and drink flown-in vodka served by flown-in waiters who will be flown out immediately when the banquet is over.

The whole thing is almost as grand as a dinner I went to in

Italy where the footman behind every chair put on new gloves for every course and a new jacket for coffee.

I know that long private discussions and meetings lie behind this evening, that great achievements and catastrophes are negotiated by a few people in private rooms, but tonight everything still seems to be unresolved. The pact to be signed the next morning, for which the whole world is waiting, is still not certain.

Surely our future is not going to be decided over the dessert?

Everyone seems to be taking part in a parlor game.

A horrible suspicion dawns on me. That the seriousness with which journalists report the meetings of these men is either another kind of game or deliberate manipulation of the facts.

To me it looks like a first-night party at the Norwegian Theatre.

The same noncommittal speeches and words and toasts and promises that mean nothing.

Could it be that the whole world is taking part in the same performance? A small number of people in leading roles; in lesser but very important ones, the reporters. Then there are all the rest of us, who are the audience.

And the victims.

I AM A WANDERER. EVEN WHEN I THINK I HAVE GROWN roots, suddenly, the next day, I find myself on the way to another city, a different country. But sooner or later, I am always home again.

On the stage in Oslo, or in Sweden with Ingmar.

My agent, Paul, thinks it would be better for my international career if I were to settle down in California.

He produces pictures of his grandchildren and shows them to me, is full of pride taking guests around his house and his garden, relaxes happily when he is with his family, all of whom are close to him.

I want him to recognize the same needs in me. He finds it difficult to understand that I can regard a stage part at home in Norway to be as essential as anything he can offer me.

Paul and I have dinner with his daughter's oldest son. The boy looks at Paul with critical eyes behind round spectacles. "You ought to put a jacket on at table," the little one says. His grandfather smiles so broadly and proudly and though the air in the room is quivering with heat, he finds a jacket and puts it on, and he is more genial and happy than I have ever seen him at any of his clients' gala premieres.

In my Beverly Hills villa, Jerry Brown tells me about his life as a monk. For several years he lived a very spartan life in a strict monastery. He talks about God and his beliefs, tells of all the good things that he would like to do when he gets political power. Jerry buries a bird in our garden. It has flown against the window and died almost immediately. He holds it in his hand and believes it is an omen. I don't know of what. Today he is governor of California and someday, perhaps, he will be President.

I attend political dinners, think at times that people at

them resemble dolls you wind up: heads turning regularly from one side to another irrespective of what they are saying. Smiles that never leave the face—nor do they reach the eyes.

Sundays beside the swimming pool; friends who come and go. Some have traveled all the way from Norway and now lie in the sun feeling good.

Dinner at Emily's home. She is my press secretary, friend and substitute mother over here. Her two dogs, both of them small and surly, sit at the table wearing bows. Her mother, who is ninety, and whom Emily pats on the cheek all the time, is clearly the center of her world.

I sit on a sofa in a hotel room, saying goodbye to a man I can no longer live with. I am crying and he is crying. For an instant I glance up. On the wall in front of us there is a mirror. He stares into it, arranging the hair over his forehead while he makes sniffing noises.

Someone takes my hand and reads the future in its lines. I am to have two difficult years and then the best period of my life. Everything he tells me I believe.

I meet a world-renowned astrologer at a party. He holds my arm in a tight grip and looks intently at me, as he tells me I'm an enormously interesting personality; he simply must chart my horoscope. Very flattered, I agree—and believe every word he says: I am to have two fantastically happy years, and then a really difficult one. He asks me for two hundred dollars. He makes it cheap, he says, because he is my friend.

I spend long lonely nights sitting up in bed, eating spaghetti and spilling red sauce on the quilt, or make expensive telephone calls home, or select a program on one of the thirteen television channels.

At work, on the street, in my social life, sooner or later I run into all the names I have read about, all the faces I have seen pictured.

Vanessa Redgrave rings my doorbell and talks about revolution for two hours without once looking at me. I begin to feel nervous. She never lets me get a word in. She asks me to write a check—they are going to build a school in London to train new revolutionary leaders. I say that I would prefer to go into it a bit more; has she by any chance a brochure I could study on my own? She looks me in the face for the first time and tells me they need money *now*. I ask if she thinks the revolution will be a bloody one, and she replies that because of their opponents' aggressiveness, bloodshed is unavoidable. Now she doesn't take her eyes off my face. With stiff fingers, I fumble with my checkbook. I am thinking that her stomach is full of my lunch, that she is much taller than I, and perhaps she can see that I am frightened of her. Her voice tells me to make the check for as large an amount as possible. Speechlessly I watch her walk out the door clutching my check in her hand. An hour later I send her a telegram, asking her to transfer the money to Amnesty International.

Jane Fonda wins an Oscar. The next morning, while I read about her great triumph in the newspapers, she phones me to say that she has managed to find the name and telephone number of a wonderful speech therapist: "I heard you were looking for one." And then she warmly wishes me good luck.

The sewing circle is having cocktails all over Hollywood. Their best memory is an evening with Rock Hudson. After having brought them to Disneyland on his day off, he makes a lovely supper, only for them. Shows them around his beautiful house, unlike anything they know in Norway. Five Norwegian girls sit on a big terrace in the home of one of the heroes of their youth, watching night fall over Los Angeles.

I have dinner with a producer and his wife. While we eat, we stare at three television sets at once. He loves football, and three games are being shown on three different channels.

I play film star with my child and jump with her fully dressed into the swimming pool, because we've read they do this here.

The warmth of the people I meet in Hollywood is unique. The hospitality, the generosity.

Linn is as welcome as I in every home. Thanksgiving and Christmas and other holidays become for us a succession of visits from one house to another where everybody with the same kindness takes care of two who are living far from their own country.

But Los Angeles can also be frightening, when there is a ring at the door and a policeman outside tells me that I must not let Linn play alone on the street. Or when a friend comes to see us and is shocked that I let Linn answer the door.

It is frightening, because there is so much I don't understand, experiences I can't share. More drugs, more shattered dreams, tired eyes, sick minds, than I have seen anywhere else. Superficiality and flattery. Lines whose hardness can no longer be hidden by make-up. Bitterness and disappointment permanently etched into a face that is carefully painted and masked with powder and creams.

I often long to be there in California—but when I am living there, I long even more to be home.

SHE GREW UP IN A COUNTRY WHERE THE LIGHT HAD A
blue tone.

For many years she saw the seasons give constant new faces
to the landscape she lived in. Four times every year she regis-
tered the change around her.

A little girl—a winter day—with wool clothing between
herself and the cold—bending her back to be protected
against the wind—freezing as if she were living in the middle
of a snowball.

Later in life she carried this feeling within her.

In the same way that she retained the happiness of the first
day when she was allowed to go out in knee-length stockings
and, if she was really lucky, in short sleeves, with a coat over
her arm, "just in case."

The tree, for so many months with its naked, almost black,
branches outside her window, transformed itself in the course
of a few days into a veil of green that hid the rest of the world
from her when she peeped out.

And the beauty of the autumn.

Through all her adult life this was the season in which she
felt most at home; even as a child she loved autumn most.

When the leaves took on the most wonderful golden colors
—as if God wanted to adorn them one last time before they fell
and died and were swept away by the wind.

I HAVE GONE ASTRAY IN THE WHITE HOUSE. I WALK DOWN corridors that lie dark in the night. Past security agents and secretaries sitting at telephones.

Only the President's Oval Office is empty and in semi-darkness.

I see family pictures on the walls and gilt on the chairs.

A door is ajar; I peer into a bathroom much smaller than mine at home. But here is a telephone: four buttons he can press for four advisers, if anything has to be decided while he is sitting there.

Today, when I see photographs of the ex-President, I wonder what these buttons meant to him—if he misses them and what they signified.

Another time and another place I see a royal bed and a royal bedroom, but there is no king.

The bed is much narrower than mine at home, and I see a pair of rather worn slippers, and family pictures on the walls, and no gilt on the chairs.

On the night table lies a book I have just finished reading. Now when I see pictures of this king in the newspapers my feelings for him are warmed by the memory of his slippers.

One autumn I invite Mamma and my sister to Tokyo, which is my birthplace. Where Mamma almost forty years ago had been her happiest and most youthful.

She is so full of expectation when we set out. Looks forward to speaking Japanese, wandering on the old paths, finding the house in the park which was our home—showing her daughters where she had lived her happiness.

We are at a gas station. It is raining. We are surrounded by photographers, who have followed us on our search for my first home. Now they are bored and impatient. My sister is freezing. I am afraid that my newly set hair will be destroyed.

In the midst of us all stands Mamma, alone and bewildered. She looks at the walls all around us, the cars, the pumps. Almost to herself she says, "But we used to live here. It *must* have been here."

The memory of Mamma, homeless, is much clearer than the picture published in the papers the next day.

Mamma who, laughing, flings out her arms as though she jokingly regrets how everything that once was she exists no longer.

MASKS

I AM IN NEW YORK AND FOR FOUR MONTHS I AM GOING to work as Nora in *A Doll's House.*

It is my third time: shortly after the break with Ingmar I played her in a radio dramatization in Norway; last year I was Nora in Oslo, and then toured the country by bus with the production. This time it is Lincoln Center in New York.

Scenes from a Marriage has recently premiered, and I have the experience of coming to New York already a success. When I went to Hollywood for the first time I ended up as a cover story in *Time;* now it is *Newsweek.* Tickets to the entire run have been sold out a week before the premier. The theatre's public relations office has over a hundred requests for interviews. I ask them to set a limit.

This is perhaps the last time I will play Nora, and I want to devote myself to her. Through her try to discover where I stand as a woman today.

I am keeping a diary, or rather writing on scraps of paper, which I leave all over the place.

It still happens (although I kick myself inwardly) that I am with a man and find myself apologizing for my strength. Because I see him as the weaker, and perhaps therefore frightened by that strength.

I look him in the eyes as I praise his progress and minimize my own.

I am privileged—and reflect on it with a kind of shame every day when I am driven to the theatre, after having had breakfast rolled in on a hot table, been bowed in and out of the elevator, accompanied to the car with an umbrella if it is raining.

I am what many would call privileged, but I have long since discovered that success in the human sense cannot be found in these surroundings.

The best thing that can come with success is the knowledge that it is nothing to long for.

I will never forget the loneliness I knew as a child.

For a period of my life I hid behind a mask. Did not want to acknowledge any longing.

Now it is part of me—something I can share.

Both the loneliness and the longing.

I slip into a performance of *Scenes from a Marriage*. Want to experience it with an American audience. I tingle a little with pride as I stand in the long line, a part of all those people who are going in to see my film.

Marianne is so impatient in her love. I see her more clearly now than when I played her.

The parting with Johan: She clings to her beloved and thinks that by doing this she will be able to keep him. She does not accept in her heart that everything is constantly in movement—including love—and therefore subject to the law of change.

I cry when Johan leaves, as does the woman next to me in the darkness of the theatre. Know exactly how it feels when a door slams shut. A car drives off. The silence afterward, which more clearly than anything else announces that all hope is gone. It is over.

For many years Marianne has allowed part of herself to lie unused. All that a traditional upbringing has stifled. Her view of life has been built on convention and lack of fantasy; love to a great extent has been a feeling of dependency. She has tried to ground her life on another human being in the optimistic belief that he had enough strength for them both.

She has relaxed inside what she hoped he felt for her.
Now it is silence. He has left her.

Raging and helpless, Marianne screams out her anguish.
Which is my anguish. Which the woman next to me also
recognizes.

Marianne hides herself deep, deep under a quilt; decides
never to come out again. She will never again be quite the
same.

Some do what Nora did. Slam the door behind them.
Others, like Marianne, peer out from under a bedspread,
which for hours has listened to their sobbing.

A change has taken place. The old life is over. The new is
in its beginning.

I want so much the experience—the ability—to hold one
hand throughout life. Without demanding.

But I am standing in my own way. All of me is there as a
huge padlocked cargo of terror, as forgotten chapters which
should be remembered, as fear of being alone.

All the insecurity that inhabits the person called Liv.

Nora stands in the door and says: "I don't know what will
become of me. I don't know where I am going. I only know
that I can no longer bother about what others say. I must find
my own way."

Is this not where life's possibilities lie? Not necessarily to
arrive, but *always* to be on the *way,* in *movement.*

Also in love.

Also with the same hand in mine—if I am lucky.

Performing *A Doll's House* in a foreign language after
having played it in Norwegian is extremely difficult for me. I
set my alarm for 5 a.m. Read and read. Make a lot of changes
in the translation because Nora's words are so full of meaning

for me. I know them so well, and I think the English translation has missed a lot of what is Nora's distinctive quality.

One of the problems I have is "washing" the Norwegian text from my head. It is essential for me now to think in English, and if I cannot leave the Norwegian associations behind me, I will never be able to manage this.

Here, I have to acquire a new set of images, a new grid of references. Nora in New York can never be the same as Nora in Oslo.

We have been given three weeks for rehearsal. At home I am used to having two months. In my own language.

In the evenings I watch television. I cannot go out at night when the alarm clock is set for 5 a.m. The advertisements which interrupt programs every ten minutes—sometimes more frequently—make me furious in behalf of my sex.

Women are urged to change their scent, cream their hands, wash their hair in special herbs, make up their faces beyond recognition, improve their breasts—all in order to catch and/or keep a man.

I used to want to lodge in someone's pocket and be able to jump in and out whenever it suited me. Now I go around listening for cries from women who I imagine are locked in others' pockets.

I realize I was brought up to be the person others wanted me to be, so that they would like me and not be bothered by my presence.

That person was not me.

When I began to be *me,* I felt that I had more to give.

Life was richer.

I am trying to eliminate all the bad conscience caused by things of no significance that stand in the way of what I really believe in.

Nora says to Helmer: "But I have lived only to be your plaything. And you wanted it that way."

The premiere is over and things go well for me. Newspapers, radio and television want interviews. People I know only by name telephone and invite me to their homes.

In a strange way I don't feel part of it all.

All the beautiful words I read. I think: Oh, what beautiful words! I do hope they'll read them back home in Norway.

But it isn't *me*. I am the person who is longing for her child, for the people she loves, for her home.

I am the person who worries about what will happen after the premiere. Whether she will get more work in the future. Whether she is a bad mother.

The taste of success lasts only one day. It is a relief when it comes after a period of intense work. It is good. But now failure is that much closer, because success can only bear a greater one—or a failure.

I want to express something about humanity in my work—something with which one can identify, and which will convey the message that it is possible for people to "belong." That it is possible to long for that. So that those who have always felt on the outside can understand that we experience it together. The longing.

Scenes from a Marriage was an opportunity I had to reach others because so many people recognized themselves in it—even if briefly.

The film is about communication, about living with another human being, about seeing others as they are, not as a mask which passes for the real person.

No relationship between people is perfect.

No violins play when someone I love kisses me. Hollywood's "happy ending" is a manufactured product which never finds its equal in real life. A dream world that is treacherous because it incites people to march off to ever new tunes. Fully believing that this time they have found "the right one."

When Marianne and Johan divorce, they discover bonds far stronger than the marriage contract. They know that they belong to each other in an indefinable way, because in their freedom from each other they have learned something about themselves—they know themselves a little better.

They are not perfect. Their friendship is not perfect friendship. They have many wounds. But they have survived.

And found each other again when they thought everything was over.

Marianne is always thinking about love, is worried because she cannot make her feeling resemble what she believes it ought to be.

"What is love?" "Is this love that I have?"

The end of the film provides the answer:

The tenderness between the two—that they have each other now.

In a simple happiness.

That is love. Their kind of love.

The rest is fantasy.

I remember Kristina and Karl Oskar in *The Emigrants*. They never spoke to each other about feelings. Nor do I think they thought much about it. But when Kristina lay dying thousands of miles from her homeland, Karl Oskar sat on the edge of her bed, held her hand and said so quietly and with such certainty: "You and I are the best of friends."

More beautifully it cannot be said.

A Doll's House previews in Philadelphia for three weeks. We rehearse during the day and perform in the evening.

I want the public to see through Nora's mask, the way she plays with her surroundings.

I want the doll to be seen dancing.

Some actors work by imagining themselves into the details of the character. My feeling is that the challenge lies in being able to depict what is real in the moment. The joy I feel then resembles what I feel when I am writing.

I write a role, a character. I try to tell everything I know about her on the stage. At that moment the actress is close to the author. What I do onstage cannot be based on *my* feelings alone, for then I might be fantastically good one evening, but because it was all *my* emotion, I wouldn't know what made me laugh and cry, and I couldn't reproduce it at the next performance.

I have to know what I do with Nora. In a sense stand behind her—present her: do you recognize this woman?

We are sitting in a hotel room. I am happy each time the cast gets together after a performance. This is such a dark and dreary place where we live. I am afraid at night. Sleep with the light on. Keep hearing sounds I cannot identify. Strange and threatening-looking people are loitering outside on the streets.

One of the girls goes to her room to fetch something. She doesn't return. We find her naked on the bed, tied, gagged and raped. A man was in the bathroom when she came in, hiding behind the shower curtain. Pulled it aside—was there—without clothes, a black hood over his head, and with a bread knife in his hand.

I help her pull on her sweater and slacks. The police are waiting in the corridor. She is going to be questioned and taken to the hospital to be examined. A woman has to prove that she has been raped before a charge is taken seriously.

The knife is lying on the floor, as is his mask, and the gag, made of her torn pillowcase, hangs damp around her neck. But that is insufficient evidence.

She isn't crying. But I am not going to forget her eyes— they speak a language I do not recognize.

That night we all sleep together; in my room there are five of us. The next day we move to a different hotel.

The theatre has assigned a secretary to me, Debbie. She is half my size, but tough and energetic, and keeps at a distance people I do not wish to see.

The hairdresser's name is Roy. One day I arrive at my dressing room, formerly cold and impersonal, and find it decorated with rugs and pillows in a flowered pattern. There is a make-up cape of the same material, which he has made for me, hanging over the chair.

"This is your room," he says. "You can take everything with you to future dressing rooms, and it will always be the same room."

My room.

For a time there is an armed policeman outside.

During the night a bodyguard keeps watch in my living room. In the apartment there are wires strung in all directions; an alarm goes off each time a slight breeze brings two wires into contact. We dare not open the windows. Even so, there are frequent false alarms. Four big men rushing in with drawn pistols. For a time I sleep only a few hours each night.

Linn, who is visiting, says that she is never coming to America again.

All my life I have read that a mother should and must be home with her child.

My guilt is deep-seated. Bad conscience is part of my everyday life. I am afraid that I am doing Linn an injustice.

But at the same time I think that she gets more from me precisely because of my happiness in a profession I love, which gives me such stimulation.

Ingmar is in New York. He seems very out of place here. When one knows him as I do, and observes him unnoticed, he seems so endlessly vulnerable. In the middle of the street, surrounded by traffic and—if one wants to look at them that way—threatening skyscrapers. Far from the tranquillity and routine of Fårö and its peaceful wanderings.

He always touches the mother in me. The way he did when I was twenty-five and knew almost nothing about him.

Goethe wrote that placed face to face with one's superior, one's ego can do nothing but declare love.

For me it is not that way:

—Ingmar in the lobby of the Hotel Pierre, an uncertain smile around his mouth as he is bowed into an elevator.

—Linn, who grabs my hand, giving me a look that asks me to tell her what she should do.

—A man I love, whose voice is choked as he speaks, trying to hold back the tears he doesn't want me to see.

—Mamma, when she sails into a premiere, defenseless in all her pride, because she cannot understand that everyone may not share her enthusiasm in the daughter's work.

—My best friend, who writes a long letter about nothing, and in a postscript casually mentions that the man she has been living with for many years has suddenly married someone else.

Pictures of my beloved ones, when I want to embrace them, shelter them, caress them and thank them because they are completely vulnerable—*these* are the pictures that arouse my love.

There are women who would certainly be happier if they lived alone, but they have the feeling they must own somebody and through this show that they have value.

If they feel lonely, part of their loneliness comes from a sense that there is something missing, because the society looks down on them as if they are playing a bad role: they haven't found a partner. They are not living in "twoness."

I believe that it is sometimes less difficult to wake up and feel that I am alone when I really *am,* than to wake up with someone else and be lonely.

I hope that two people can grow together, side by side, and bring joy to each other. Without one having to be crushed so that the other may stay strong.

Perhaps maturing is also to let others *be.*

To allow myself to be what I am.

"No one will sacrifice his honor for love," says Helmer. And Nora replies: "Millions of women have."

I ask Sam Waterston, who is playing Helmer, if he would be willing to give up his profession for a woman if for some reason doing this were essential for continued relationship. Sam doesn't think so, and asks if I would.

"Yes, I could." I think about it. "I believe many women do, because we have such belief that love is important."

"But don't you value yourself more?" Sam asks.

"That is what we do. We can give up our profession because we value what we *are.*"

To live in a state of uncertainty is shattering and hard. But it is easier now that I accept this as a part of life. To live *with* it, not despite it.

I receive the prize as the year's best actress from the New York critics. Barbara, who plays Kristina, lends me a dress. (I left Norway in a hurry, and I packed all the wrong things.)

Her dress has a faint smell of incense. She doesn't drink, eats only vegetables, meditates often and for long periods, and takes life and her place in it very seriously.

(Two months later she is killed in the street. The murderer is unknown, as is the motive.)

Erland Josephson has arrived from Sweden to receive an award for Ingmar.

Together with friends, we do the town. Erland has never been in New York before.

I am wearing a hat for the first time in many years. And everything that happens to me throughout the evening I experience from a distance, as if it is not me, but someone in a strange hat, and Barbara's dress.

I am having success and everything assumes a proportion unrelated to me.

A bodyguard sits in my living room, and shows his revolver to anyone who asks.

The theatre is packed every night. I try to play Nora as if Liv weren't involved in so many other things.

When as a child I acted, the only reality that existed was the pleasure of the stage. The only happiness. I never cared whether I was sharing my own experience with others.

I painted pictures—they just happened—and it never occurred to me that people and trees and houses should be depicted in any particular way if others were to recognize them and like them.

The picture was me. The role was me.

As an adult actress, this is what I want: that Nora plays

Nora. In the best moments it happens. The finest compliment I received in the United States came from a writer who quoted Zen: "You have allowed the cloth to weave the cloth."

On stage Sam and I have a fine contact. Sometimes we feel that the public is part of this and plays with us: together we observe Nora and Helmer. We are without inhibitions and give and take from each other.

The limitation: to have only oneself as an instrument, as a means of expression.

For me it is impossible and without interest merely to go through a complete change of personality from role to role.

There are days when, during a rehearsal or a performance, unknown secrets within myself come forward, sparked by the shaping of a role, a dialogue with a fictitious character. The elation of a tiny advance. Adding to one's instrument.

I am on the stage, I am Nora, and suddenly discover that she has borrowed life from Queen Christina, whom I have previously portrayed. Nora has movements she did not have the first time I played the part, nuances in the voice I had not previously associated with her—but which emerged from the interaction between me and the Swedish queen.

It is as if every new role becomes a summary of previous ones.

I love Nora. She is beautiful, and perfectly drawn by Ibsen.

Her need to be accepted. Her fear of presenting herself as she really is.

A woman who says one thing and means something quite different. Who wants to be friends with, and liked by, everyone. Who exclaims, "Don't be angry with me!" the moment she senses she might have said something that could offend. And who all the while lives her secret life, and with strength and determination conducts financial transactions (unusual for a woman in those days) in order to save her husband's life.

This woman, who uses and manipulates those around her while at the same time wanting to help and love them, refuses to do something she feels is morally repugnant to her when the decisive moment comes. It is beyond her imagination to conceive of exploiting the situation when Dr. Rank declares his love and begs to give her the money she so badly needs.

Like Helmer, Nora is one of society's victims. She behaves in a way one would expect of a woman, of a wife, of a doll child.

She plays her part just as Helmer plays his. Neither of them gives the other a chance, because they are always in service to the other's role.

When she finally *sees,* she also understands that the anger she feels over everything that is false between them is directed just as much against herself as against him. Her responsibility was as great as his. She hopes that the change will also take place in him—not for her sake, but for his own.

Not because he is threatened by a new Nora, who shows a strength he doesn't comprehend, and which frightens him, but because he has discovered a new human being whose motives he may learn to understand.

I believe that Nora's most beautiful declaration and act of love is leaving her husband.

She says goodbye to everything that is familiar and secure. She does not walk through the door to find somebody else to live with and for; she is leaving the house more insecure than she ever realized she could be. But she hopes to find out who she is and why she is.

In this there is a great freedom: the knowledge that I have to part with my present life. I don't know for what. For myself. To be something more than I am now.

About ten times Nora exclaims: "Oh, I am so happy!" I choose to have her say it without joy—and the last time with sorrow, anxiety and longing. A critic states that I am trying to help Ibsen, so that the farewell in the final act will not come as such a shock. But I am sure Ibsen was aware of what he was doing. Do we need to go around repeating constantly that we are so happy if we really are?

Nora is strong, even in the first act: think of the joy with which she tells her friend about the long nights when she locks herself in and works.

Nora is lonely. When the doorbell rings she says to Kristina: "It's no one for me."

In the first acts Nora is not just the songbird and the squirrel; neither is she pure wisdom and feminine strength in the last.

To me, Helmer's and Nora's last scene is not a bravura number for Nora. That would be too easy. This is not how we leave someone we have loved, and presumably still love. It is not with fanfare and the sound of drums that we walk away from the familiar and go out into a new and strange world. With so little knowledge.

It is a little girl who slams the door behind her. A little girl in the process of growing up.

Onstage what I am acting is reality for me. In the same way that my reality is acting. Each is a part of the whole.

Nora says: "First and foremost I am a human being."

I am a woman—a single career woman with a child.

My life has been filled with all a human being can expect—and much more.

I have loved and been loved. I have known pain and sorrow, but also happiness far greater than I ever dreamed of as a young girl.

I have never been hungry; only at certain times did I have to count my money to see whether I could afford butter instead of margarine.

Sometimes I am happy and wake up in the morning and smile at a man I have the peace to love.

I am constantly living in a state of change, although deep inside I am "a young girl who refuses to die."

We who are alive at this moment are only an infinitesimal part of something that has existed for eternity and will continue when there is no longer anything to show that earth existed.

Still, we must feel and believe that we are all.

That is our responsibility—not only to ourselves but to everything and everyone with which we share our time here.

What is change?

Is it something that happens inside me? Or is it something I experience in other people?

Is it perhaps an even stronger conscious drive, and if so, where does it lead?

What am I striving for?

To become the best possible human being? Or the best artist?

What do I really want to do with what I have achieved?

What will I do with the change?

Maybe it isn't so important to know.

Maybe it isn't so important to arrive.

On April 20, 1975, I play Nora for the last time in New York. After two performances on Sunday I put myself on the plane, en route to Sweden to work with Ingmar.

THE FILM IS EXTRAORDINARY IN MANY WAYS. IT DEALS with death. Loneliness. Anxiety. It tells the story of a woman of my age who will soon reach the crossroads, where the middle-aged person departs the young woman. Anxiety has become a part of her everyday life, but she is not able to accept it. She cannot live with it, and decides to take her life.

In brief scenes the camera focuses on her professional life, her private life, her attempt at suicide; the final segment follows her to the hospital, where she confronts herself through dreams and through confessions to a good friend.

During the takes I sit with a yellow notebook and write down what I see and hear. When I read through it later I realize that much of it is meaningless except to me, who can recall and relate to the circumstances. People in films have a special jargon incomprehensible to an outsider. But I have collected a number of these notes because they reveal something that is important to me.

Day 1

We rent two studios at the Swedish Film Institute. In one they have built Jenny's childhood home, where her grandparents now live alone.

I am Jenny.

On this set everything is in hues of green. The place is cluttered with knickknacks and antiques, and is attractive in the secure and overstuffed way that kind of home tends to be. When Jenny's dreams take her back, the apartment has changed character through lighting, dimming of colors and an almost imperceptible rearrangement of furniture.

The second studio contains Jenny's sickbed in a small, white, impersonal room. There is also her office, and the corridors she runs through when she is in that borderline territory between life and death.

When we are not shooting we choose the grandfather's library to sit in: Ingmar reclining on a brown leather sofa, dressed in the same shirts and sweaters and pants and slippers that in all the years I have known him have not changed in style. When the old ones wear out they are replaced by replicas.

Usually I sit curled up in an enormous easy chair with my tape recorder. I seldom go to the studio without it. I love to find a little corner and quiet, quiet, listen to music. During this film it is mostly Albinoni.

We are talking about being ourselves, and I ask Ingmar if he knows any people who really *live* what they *are*.

Without a flicker of hesitation he answers, "Yes, I do."

This obvious exaggeration leaves me speechless.

An image suddenly appears. Ingmar and I a long time ago at the Copenhagen airport. He hates traveling and is apprehensive—all the people, all the noise. He panics; feels a strong urge to return home, back to the security of Fårö. The flight is delayed, and he takes an elevator down to the men's room. I wait close by at a table. After a while the elevator door opens and Ingmar comes out. He has his little cap on his head, and there is a faint smile of pride. Here is someone who has overcome his phobia, gone into a strange elevator, into a strange toilet, and made it back all by himself. He approaches me, his back stooped just a little. The faint smile has gone, but the anxious expression in his eyes is no longer so impelling, and I know that the trip will continue.

Linn and her half-brother, Daniel, come to the filming almost every day. Ingmar is faced with a conflict between his role as a father and that of director. Sometimes he goes blank in one of these roles because he feels he cannot manage the other.

Our new dog, Sivan, is lying in my dressing room. She is a golden retriever, wild and undisciplined, and devours all shoes and socks she can find. Takes little nibbles from my costumes, wets the floor when she is greeting Ingmar—and rips my letters to shreds.

Day 2

Confidence is important in filming. An actor who feels secure with the director, who in turn trusts the actor, will achieve much more in this working partnership than when such a relationship does not exist.

Ingmar talks about how important it is for him as a director to have security. How quickly he becomes apprehensive when he feels that he is losing contact with the actor—when they have no communication, no recognition between them. Then things close in. It is in such moments one can witness one of his famous fits of rage.

The part I am now playing is written for me. In this lies my security and also Ingmar's. We both feel that I can identify with Jenny. That I can transform Jenny into Liv.

Build on my own experience, on that of others—on everything I have heard and seen in thirty-six years.

The day Ingmar gives me the manuscript he also gives me the right to feel that henceforward I understand the part best. She becomes my reality as much as she is Ingmar's. With his help, genius, his sensibility in listening and looking, I know that my knowledge of her will be captured by the camera.

To film with Ingmar is stretches of happiness when everything feels real.

Day 3

The rooms are green. Chairs, walls, plants, objects, everything there is in some shade of green. With a few lamps that give off light and create contrasting shadows, Sven Nykvist, the cinematographer, establishes an atmosphere of bygone days.

Gunnar Bjornstrand and Aino Taube play my grandparents. I am watching them play a scene.

Gunnar drags his feet in slippers that are too big. Aino is wearing socks. It is night, and grandfather has got up to wind the clock. He is anxious. He is afraid of dying. He knows that he soon *must* die, and sees an omen in the clock that has stopped. Aino consoles him, embraces him, chides him a little, and jokes with him.

I think of my own grandmother, who died so long ago, and whom I still miss.

I also think about my own death. It seems much closer now than it was only a few years ago.

I believe in God, and know that if I really could believe in eternal life there would be no death and no fear.

But that is a spiritual experience which is not as yet mine. All around me I see evidence that there is no death. After winter comes the spring, but if I am not part of it, I am unable to experience it as life.

My fear of death limits me. Leaves me open to it.

Day 4

It is Sunday and I am lying on the sheet I bought in America that is covered with roses and apples and edged with lace. Below in the garden, Linn is playing with her dog. It is only 8 a.m. She is laughing and shouting, and I know the neighbors are trying to sleep. But I take no action; they play their radio and television at night when *I* want to sleep.

I lie on my roses without thorns, and work: learn a long

monologue in which Jenny tells her husband that she is thinking of taking her life.

Linn comes in and tells me what the puppy has learned, and I hear her voice saying that it has just climbed the stairs by itself for the first time, while inside me Jenny is saying in a tired voice that in a little while she is going to take a hundred sleeping pills and die.

I know that in a few days when I speak these lines before the camera I will have tears in my eyes because I will suddenly remember Linn the way she is now: in a gym outfit and milk mustache, eagerly trying to make contact, entirely unaware that I hear almost nothing of what she is saying.

Day 5

Sometimes Ingmar wears one blue and one yellow sock—usually on the first day of filming. We are all convinced this will bring luck to our work.

Ingmar eats alone. His lunch consists of a hard-boiled egg, a piece of toast with strawberry jam, and a bowl of sour cream. On a small table in the studio there is a reserve of crackers, chocolate and soda.

He and I walk up and down the corridor, discussing Jenny's depression. Nobody around her recognizes it until it is too late.

Her ability to experience has narrowed; the contrast between the levels of intensity with which she formerly encountered music, beauty, other people, and what she now feels, has sharpened.

Jenny has been clever. She has managed to live a part, live behind a mask, conceal a pain. Sometimes it has taken a physical form, for which she has bought pills and salves at the pharmacy. But mostly she has been in full control.

She has tried to close her eyes to fear and has been success-

ful until this moment when she is confronted with her childhood surroundings.

Here the structure collapses—here her defenses no longer
work.

In these safe rooms of childhood there are no rational ex-
planations when fear follows. The threat exists where the
means do not exist to fight it.

I think it logical that Jenny never knew she wanted to die
before she went home to visit her grandparents.

Day 6

I see myself as a sieve. Everyone's feelings flow through
me, but I am never able to retain them.

In the evening I am put aside empty—only to be inundated
the next day with new emotions.

I am childish. Settle back in happiness when I am praised.

"I couldn't have made this film without you," Ingmar says
after we have completed a scene. "In any case, it would have
been entirely different."

There is a lot in him I don't know about—although I think
I can sense most.

But what he *wants* I feel distinctly: there I recognize myself in him.

That is my fortune as an actress.

His women, whom I always see as real, become a natural
part of me. Without my believing that they are created in my
likeness. Even if he gives me a role that seems unfamiliar to
me, I know that while he was writing, he knew I could understand the character—that I have a backlog of experience
which can be utilized when her experiences are to be un-
folded.

Sometimes we surprise each other. That is the best of all.

I also see myself a shameless and greedy collector of smiles and tears, emotions and expressions, both my own and those I see in others. For later use in work.

Day 7

It has been a late evening—for me in any case, since I have to get up at five-thirty. Cilla, the make-up artist, puts drops in my eyes—a blue water that transforms the reddest eyes into marvels of clarity.

Last night I wore a low-cut dress and a short wig, neither of which is part of my usual wardrobe. For the first time in ages people said, "You are too young to possibly remember . . ."

Today we talk about death, motivated by the picture. Aino lost both her husband and her mother within a short period of time. She tells us about her mother, who during her illness never felt fear for herself. Only sadness and a kind of futile rage because she had to leave her daughter. Aino's husband died after a long and painful illness. In his last months she would tie her wrist to his at night, so that she would know if he awoke or was disturbed in his sleep.

Love is also this.

We talk about our fear of death. In smaller communities death is a more visible part of everyday life. A coffin is carried through narrow streets, with the people of the village following. A nicer and more personal way to say goodbye. People close to the one who has gone, not cars.

Today's scene shows Jenny as she wakes from two days' deep sleep. She has slept and slept, escaping her torment as best she can. A few years ago I could not have played that scene. I would have tried to do too much, complicated it, been tense and nervous. Now I joke in the breaks and I resume my concentration with the others when Ingmar says, "Action!"

No studio in the world is as silent as his when the red light for "filming in progress" is on.

I want to jump and dance when it is finished and we go for coffee.

I feel very proud.

I appear quite calm, and discuss recipes with Cilla, while inside me I sing: "I can do it! I can do it!"

Day 8

Today we shall film the suicide scene. Ingmar has ordered facsimiles of real sleeping tablets. The manufacturer promises that they will be filled with grape-flavored sugar. There are a hundred of them, a whole bottle full.

I am almost sick with fear, imagine that the manufacturer has made a mistake, that perhaps they contain the real thing after all.

In the studio the atmosphere is depressed; everyone is obviously nervous. Ingmar gives me loose directions and says, "Now we will see what happens."

"Action!"

I don't know how I will do it. I can hardly take an aspirin without coughing and clearing my throat, and now I have to swallow a hundred pills.

Jenny arranges the bedcover, fluffs up two pillows and fixes them nicely so that her head can rest on them, pulls down the shade, locks the door, straightens out the covers once more, sits down on the edge of the bed, fills a glass with soda, opens the medicine bottle, puts two, three pills in her hand, swallows with a little difficulty. Next time there are more in the palm. She stuffs them into her mouth, drinks. Suddenly Jenny's hand begins to tremble so violently that the glass knocks against my teeth—and while *Jenny* is trying to take her life *I* know how it feels.

The long preparation, the strange stillness Jenny and I are doing it together. I experience it at the same time as I am standing outside, watching. I am living through a suicide.

Ten, twenty pills in my mouth at a time go down easily. Jenny becomes increasingly agitated, but the countenance remains calm. She sits for a while looking at the empty bottle, shakes her head, then she lies down and rests her head against the pillows she has arranged. For a while she lies staring at the ceiling.

It suddenly strikes me how right it would have been if she had looked at her watch, noted the time of her death—and at the same moment the thought comes to me, she does it.

It only becomes theatre when I turn my face toward the wall and *do not* die.

Afterward I feel empty. Notice that someone is crying.

Not only the actor but also the spectator can at certain times participate in unreality as if it were real.

Ingmar is quiet and subdued and says, "Well, now at least I won't have to commit suicide."

Day 9

Ingmar and I clashed today. His face looks like a cloudburst when he sees me going to lunch with a reporter. He calls me back and hisses, "I am so tired, so tired of you and your damned reporters." I hiss back, "And I am so happy because you have no say over me. That I don't have to see your face around the clock—now that I really know who you are!"

We part in anger. He goes to his office and his sour cream, and I to my interview, where I explain for the thousandth time why working with Ingmar Bergman is so fantastic.

When it is over I return to my dressing room and I burst into laughter because I see the two of us standing there in the hall shouting at each other in whispers—while the reporter, eyes aglow, is under the impression that he is witnessing a fragment of a most marvelous working relationship. I sit on the sofa, and I laugh and laugh, wondering what I will say when I meet him on the set. I will have to pretend I am unhappy, borrow the "sad eyes" at which my mother is so adept. While I am getting them ready, there is a knock on the door and he enters—and has been laughing like me, to his sour cream and strawberry jam.

We have our anger, but never let it interfere with our work.

We only hiss a little—when necessary.

The collaboration between a director and an actor, if it is a good one, is extremely intense, and very often there is a touch of aggression—usually from the actor. If you are ordered about for a whole day by a director—to walk and stand and talk, look a certain way, take the lunch break now and finish for the day now (even if spoken by a genius)—there are times when you think: Shoot the man. I want to be free, feel free. I hate him.

Then you let your anger out in small clouds of steam, and everyone knows that it doesn't mean a thing.

Day 10

Ingmar talks about his mother. Of his fear of doing something wrong when he was a child. Once when he was caught wetting his pants she put his sister's red dress on him and made him go out into the street.

He talks about his mother's diaries, which bring to life a woman the family never knew. Only after her death did they meet her as she was, through her own secret journals.

When she had only a few days left to live and was lying with a tube in her nose, she suddenly said to Ingmar, "My mother never cared for me." And she cried.

Once, when I had been to Norway on a visit, Ingmar fetched me at the airport.

"Mamma died today," he said when we were in the car.

She had had her third heart attack. The hospital wanted to

call him, but she told them, "He is so busy. Leave him alone."

When a nurse finally did call, it was too late. She was dead when he reached her bedside.

Her nails were varnished red; put on with care the day before.

"Now I have no one," he cried, and he was completely defenseless.

I knew that I could never leave him, and in a way I never have.

Day 11

We have reached an understanding, but we never talk about it. Because it could destroy something. I think that both of us have the same needs. Therefore he can use me. And I can use him because he uses me. It gives me the possibility to do what I want to do.

Day 12

One of the things I like about my profession, and that I find healthy, is that one constantly has to break oneself to pieces. Wounds do not have a chance to fester.

An older actress who is with us today tells about the fear she feels after being retired and no longer needed in the theatre. At night she wakes up screaming. Terrible nightmares destroy a sleep which through her whole life has been utterly sound.

What happens to a role is a kind of life, and now as I sit talking with my colleagues, Jenny is living inside me. So that in a way I am she; and what are her tears and fear and anger keep open in me that which I shall use to portray her.

We have a visitor from Hollywood, Charles Champlin—a wise and friendly man I know from many visits to America.

He is delighted with our working methods, which are different from those he is accustomed to in the Los Angeles studios.

While we are having coffee he interviews Ingmar. I sit beside them, listening. Ingmar talks about the romantic aura which surrounds certain actors. Filled with enthusiasm, he sings the praises of some he has heard about who come late to work, but who have so much charm; who don't learn their lines, but have fantastic charisma; who bring their love life to the studio, but about whom that is understandable, given their sensitive natures.

It is all so delightful and adventurous, and one cannot make the same demands on them as on other professionals, he says. Champlin nods and agrees. I turn red with anger. Here he meets daily a loyal group of actors who are proud of the absolute professionalism he demands of them. Not for a moment would Ingmar permit someone to do what he now smilingly condones.

Does he really know how it feels to go to bed at seven o'clock every night in order to be up before sunrise the next morning, learn a role, and be on time for make-up, appear before the camera, and look rested under his scrutiny? Does Ingmar understand why I boil when he speaks about amateurs with understanding, while from his own co-workers he demands total support?

Sometimes one gets so furious at directors, foremen, men in general. Their unbelievable lack of logic—one minute making demands on those nearest to them and the next showering admiration on the ones whose behavior is the exact opposite. How unrealistic they are in their position toward what they believe inside and what they express. In dealing with each other they have one truth, and yet they need another if they are to function at all.

One truth for conversation—another for life.

Day 14

I love close-ups. To me they are a challenge. The closer a camera comes, the more eager I am to show a completely naked face, show what is behind the skin, the eyes; inside the head. Show the thoughts that are forming.

To work with Ingmar is to go on a journey of discovery within my own self. To be able to realize all the things I dreamed of as a girl.

Discard the mask and show what is behind it.

The camera comes so close—and there is much of myself that is captured.

Closer to the audience than in any other medium—the human being is shown on the screen.

The camera meets me more exposed than the lover who thinks he has read my thoughts.

Even when I tell myself that I am expressing a role, I can never completely hide who *I* am, what *I* am.

The audience, at the moment of identification, meets a person, not a role, not an actress.

A face which confronts them directly:

This is what I know about women. This is what *I* have experienced, have seen. This is what I want to share.

It is no longer a question of make-up, of hair, of beauty.

It is an exposure that goes way beyond.

When the camera is as close as Ingmar's sometimes gets, it doesn't only show a face, but also what kind of life this face has seen.

Thoughts behind the forehead, something the face didn't know about itself, but which the public will see and recognize.

Privately we long for exactly this kind of recognition: that others should perceive what we really are, deep inside.

To make a film with Ingmar is, for me, to have this experience.

I am given a role, I am given Jenny; and I try to create a character, and he understands who she is at once. That is his genius: the identification, recognition, his fantastic eye and ear.

Day 15

Today the lighting is very complicated, and we sit in the library talking for a long time. Ingmar reminisces about light and sound. With a certain regret, he says that the sounds which surround us are entirely different from those he remembers as a child. He tells about the carts that creaked outside his window in the morning, the horses trotting in the streets, clocks that ticked loudly and struck every fifteen minutes, the wind in the stovepipes.

I myself remember the sound my shoes made in the spring when the snow had melted on the gravel on Munke Street.

Ingmar grew up with kerosene lamps; I saw street lamps being lit every evening by a man with a long stick. Neon lighting came to us much later. The lights in my childhood sparkled. The evenings were darker—another kind of dark than we have now, diffused by advertisements and shop-windows.

When I was little the windows all were much larger, and every home had different curtains. The pictures on the walls carried with them such strong suggestions for me that I took them with me into life as an experience.

In my childhood we went to lectures and saw slides from other countries. Now the world batters my daughter daily with live pictures on television.

And smells. They also are different. I remember the fragrance from coal and wood stoves.

Ingmar had a privy. He tells how the children hid underneath and looked up at all the bottoms.

I recall a friend who grew up on a small farm where we spent our summer holidays. He had never seen a flush toilet before he came to stay with us in the city. He pulled on the chain and thought it was the whole sea starting to pour into our apartment. It took hours of pleading to keep him from returning home immediately.

It seems to me that when I was a girl, the food cooked longer on the stove. There was always a smell of food—soups, sauces and cookies baking.

It smelled more then, when I was little.

Grandma's smell. And the smell of mothballs when we packed the winter clothes away. Mamma kept lavender in the linen closet. Ink in the inkwell.

Perhaps, also, because one brought so many live impressions from one's own immediate surroundings, the senses were more acute.

In my youth, it even seems to me, trees and flowers gave off more fragrance than they do today.

Day 16

We have many extras. They are my patients in a nightmare. Jenny is a doctor, and enters her office to find it full of white-clad suffering people. She pushes her way through them, stops by some, says a few words, moves on. All the while they keep reaching out, clutching at her.

Strange, warm hands touch me all over my body. It is terribly hot in the studio. I am nervous and forget my lines. Ingmar has slept badly and is impatient.

The extras give me dubious looks when we have to repeat take after take because I keep making mistakes.

Some of them sigh when I forget a line. There are mutterings among the group of white-clad strangers. "She makes mistakes all the time." "She makes mistakes."

I am furious at Ingmar, who lets me go through this, and when the bell sounds for lunch I race out of the studio. To his wife in the corridor I shout in passing that I hate her husband.

Later that afternoon I go to find Erland, a cherished colleague and confidant. I march into his room without knocking, the anger and humiliation still raging within me. Full of aggression, I tell him secrets about Ingmar, lies about him. Reveal that the truth about Ingmar's solitary lunches is a heap of tabloids he doesn't want to be caught reading.

Erland has such a strange expression on his face; doesn't look at me, doesn't answer me. There is an abrupt silence, and I turn and look in the direction where Erland's eyes are focused. Ingmar is sitting in a corner wearing a strange little smile, and looking sad.

Standing there, I die a little and exclaim, "This I can't handle!" I bolt from the room, out of the Film Institute, far out into the courtyard until I see a small crate with a lid. I crawl into it, although I am much too big, pull the lid down over me and decide to stay there for the rest of my life.

Cilla arrives, peers down at me and asks me to come out.

Erland tries to persuade me. But I never want to reappear. I will have to sit where I am forever.

Finally—after a long, long time—Ingmar comes and knocks on the lid.

He waits to open it until I whisper, "Come in." He asks me, "Do you want to be friends again?" and his face is kind.

Ullmann crawls out and work can continue.

Day 17
Ingmar, who has seen none of the film while we have been working, ran the whole thing last night.

Today the atmosphere is strained.

He has private conferences with representatives of each department. Some look pleased, others withdraw broodily to a corner.

I am nervous even before I meet Ingmar. Today Jenny is going to vacillate between life and death, between conscious and unconscious. It is one of the dream sequences, beautiful and full of imagination and challenge in the manuscript, but he hasn't talked much about these scenes—perhaps because he still hasn't completely worked out in his mind how they should be done. How alive am I? How dead? How real is death?

I have talked to people about their dreams. Most experience them as being on the brink of reality—only details separate dreams from real life: colors, shadows, sudden visions, illogical encounters.

Ingmar scolds me because I was as hoarse as a crow the first two days of filming, and now we have to repeat the whole thing. I feel guilty, although I know that it was partly due to fatigue. Immediately after arriving from America by plane— the day after my last performance on Broadway—I was sitting in the make-up chair here. Nerves and tension also played their part. A recurring throat condition has been a problem the past few years. Perhaps it is because I have been working so hard. I meet with a speech therapist after the filming every day, often for a couple of hours. I have also seen a throat specialist, who painted my poor throat, contemplated it, and put a light down it—in order to reach the conclusion that I had vocal cords like steel bands.

I promise Ingmar that I will go to the throat specialist again tomorrow and submit to new tests. Nervously, promise him that I will never again be hoarse. Then he asks me to stop eating open-faced sandwiches with my coffee. He would also prefer that I skip dinner when I get home. Casually I put my hands over my stomach, covering it, as I promise this too.

Otherwise he claims to be satisfied with my work. He feels that I understand what he wants to do with Jenny.

I am wearing Jenny's red dress, the one she has in her dreams, a long red dress, often with a red hood as well. I am sure there is an association here with the red walls in Ingmar's *Cries and Whispers*. Of which he remarked that this was the color of the soul.

Jenny comes running into an empty apartment; an eerie light illuminates her grandparents' furniture. Jenny calls for mamma, grandfather, grandmother, those closest to her. No one comes. Silence in all the rooms. She sinks down at a table, sees her own face in its shiny surface. From the shadows in a corner the Woman who symbolizes Jenny's anxiety emerges out of this dark nothingness.

Tore Segelcke, one of Norway's greatest actresses, plays this role.

She puts a shawl around my shoulders, and with infinite tenderness pulls me to her and says, "Now you mustn't be afraid any longer."

Tore is doing her first film role at the age of seventy. She is a wonderful person; everyone loves her. Ingmar says that to him she embodies all that is womanness. But in this film she does not have much of a chance to show it.

Aino also enters Jenny's dream. Ingmar remarks that something strange happens to her mouth when she is bracing herself for a close-up. Aino says, "I know, I know. That's my defense mechanism." Ingmar kindly asks, "Is this hard for you?" "When art is concerned, one doesn't bother about oneself," answers the actress.

Day 18

We talk about life. Ingmar, Gunnar, Aino and I "The older I become, the more I think about my mother," says Ingmar. "When I look at my brother, it seems it was only yesterday we were running barefoot in the garden, and I feel a fear inside me."

Gunnar remarks that death is a strange phenomenon. He himself is quite terrified of it. A man he knew went to bed when he was told that the end was near. He lay there and waited twenty years.

I have been to the doctor; a new blood test, new throat examination. Something is wrong, and I am worried. All this talk of death has affected me. In a vague way I feel that it is closer than before. Earlier I never thought about it, never understood when people would talk about their longing for life to be over.

It is afternoon. I am sitting alone listening to music. Ingmar walks by, stops for a moment and gives me a pat on the head. There is stillness between us. Then he says, "I feel as if I were on a train—first class—riding through time. It is very strange."

He sits down on his sofa, puts his legs on the table. He is wearing gray socks—just like the ones he wore five years ago, ten years ago.

"You and I have a child together," he remarks suddenly, into the air.

A flash of memory:

Linn is four weeks old. She has colic and cries and cries. Ingmar sits with her in bed. He undresses her—then himself; places her tiny body, which is stiff with cramps, against his bare stomach. She quiets down, and in each other's warmth they fall asleep.

Day 19

Over Pentecost I go to my cabin in Sandefjord. It is on the top of a high bluff. In front of me I see only the sea. I love this place. I am surrounded by space: nature, stones, trees, moss.

I can run far, far, far.

A dog, beside himself with elation, digs a hole in the earth, becomes covered with mud, almost disappears into the ground; only his tail protrudes.

Linn has secrets and hiding places. She comes home, having been in the Enchanted Forest and the White Forest— places I will never know. She tells me about Yr, her best friend, who lives somewhere far away where she cannot take me. There are bad men and good men, and Linn is leading the war between them and it is very dangerous.

My whole childhood is out there somewhere with her.

The adults sit in front of the fireplace and watch the strange configurations of the flames, feel the heat in our faces. Or we go for long walks, read, watch the days and nights come and go through the large windows.

Observe the sea, which is constantly changing.

Tiny, tiny waves that ruffle the surface of the water as if calling: "Look at me—look how big and strong I make the sea." They don't know how many millions there are of them. Then they crash on the rocks.

The clouds in the sky, the colors, the darkness which descends and envelops us.

Everything is a part of my house on the top of a bluff, somewhere in Norway.

Day 20

We are back in Stockholm. Linn is going to film today. There has been thunder in the air, and I think Ingmar has been affected by it. He is particularly angry at me because Linn has a cold. He has a deathly fear of germs, and looks at me with a wordless fury I recognize all too well. The old insecurity I used to have in similar situations blocks what I would like to say to him: that Linn has been looking forward for months to this day when she is going to film with Papa.

That she got up at five-thirty to fly from Norway to Sweden. Her anticipation in the car, the delight in her new dress and new shoes.

Now she is told that the role she was promised has been reduced to "sleeping child."

Is this her punishment for having a cold?

"She will become an actress yet," he says to me when she asks to be excused from being a "sleeping child," asks at least to be a "listening child."

Linn is learning a lot today. I know that. And I know that it hurts, and that I can do nothing to help her except be especially good to her afterward.

The sun makes an appearance when the two of us go to Skansen in the afternoon. Baby chicks and kittens in the children's zoo. A play is being presented. We sit close together on a hard bench, watching. A mother who is inwardly raging at the child's father, who can never for an instant forget his fear of disease. A little girl who looks happy.

I cook corn on the cob for dinner. Our favorite—with lots of butter and salt. We gorge ourselves. A real conversation— we take time. Afterward we have a bubble bath together, watch the news on television, discuss, hot chocolate.

In bed we sit and draw. She draws a girl who is laughing and healthy. And another who cries because she is sick.

We turn out the light. Tonight Linn is going to sleep in my bed. I set the alarm for four-thirty the next morning, so that I can learn my part then instead of now.

I don't even concern myself with what her father was thinking about when this working day was over.

Probably he just thought about his film. That, fathers are allowed to do.

Day 21

The following day the scene in Jenny's office is played. I

don't know my lines, although I have gone over them repeatedly that morning. I am desperate, and remember what Laurence Olivier said: for several years he had gone through horrible stage fright because as he started each line he couldn't remember how it ended.

I feel like an animal in a cage. Everyone realizes my predicament. They speak quietly among themselves and avoid addressing me directly.

Cilla gives me encouraging winks, but I can see in her eyes that I am a disaster. For a moment I put my head in my hands.

Ingmar's patience when the scene has to be repeated time after time because I forget my lines is not consoling me in the least.

The actor I work with in this scene has his first day of filming, and I feel that I am ruining things for him too. My nervousness is contagious.

To be alone in front of the camera. To establish the part. Show myself in it. All the lines. The constant scrutiny. The audience around to witness the defeat.

Finally Ingmar takes me by the hand, and we walk up and down in the corridor. The happenings of the previous day come flooding out with tears, and I show him the drawing Linn made in the evening.

Ingmar carefully asks for forgiveness and says that he has not had a good night's sleep for a long time. He is worried about this film. Afraid that he is going to become ill. That he won't be able to see it through.

Slowly, he leads me up to the make-up room, where Cilla is waiting to take over what is left of my face.

As I drive home, I notice something now in the city scene. More houses have armed guards at the door. Several people were killed at an embassy a couple of weeks ago. They put a man at the window and shot him in the back, in front of everyone standing in the street.

Fear has come to stay.

I can suddenly encounter death on my own street.

Day 22

Linn has been having nightmares and crawls into my bed. I lie and look at her while it is still early morning outside.

A child who wakes so differently from a grownup. A chest which is neither male nor female—only a skinny little bird's breast.

Around her mouth a smile that belongs to all of the face— very soft.

A flicker in the eyelashes from happiness when she feels that I lie with her, that I have time.

The child who pats me, who is open and tender, who falls asleep again—turns and sighs and dreams.

Day 23

We have a bona fide nurse in the studio today and I have tubes up my nose and in my arm. The actress who is going to play the part of the nurse is being instructed by the professional.

I have the same experience as when I swallowed the hundred pills. This is real. Film and reality merge. Lately I've been so preoccupied by death that everything which carries its smell has a special memory for me.

I am not afraid of dying at this moment, nonetheless I keep having these thoughts.

The atmosphere is tense. Ingmar seems troubled, and I don't know what it is. I have the feeling that he is making an effort to be friendly. When he shows me where I am supposed to go, he doesn't take my arm warmly and lightly as he usually does. His fingers have a hard and stiff grasp on me.

I think this film touches him more than any previous ones. As if he lives it, he will also be without defenses when others later judge it, see it, talk about it.

I live in an old apartment. Right across the street from Ingmar and Ingrid. They have redecorated it for me. Each room has its own color, cheerful and strong. In the bedroom are curtains from *Cries and Whispers;* in the living room the furniture from *Scenes from a Marriage.* There are posters on the walls, and in Linn's room toys from Ingrid's childhood home.

Sometimes we stand at our windows and wave at each other as we talk on the telephone. If I've been away on a short trip he'll be there, afraid that something may have happened to me. At times he'll comment, "You were burning candles in your apartment last night—well, well." Or, "Yesterday we seem to have gone to bed early."

It's like being a little girl again, when Mamma was checking on what time I came home, and with whom, and how long I spent in the hallway.

Day 24

Ingmar says, "Now I feel I have found equilibrium. Living no longer torments me."

Every time he proclaims this he believes it, because he always says it on a good day.

Erland remarks, "If it were only true! Then we wouldn't have to come here and commit suicide. And suffer and stand in the corners and feel ashamed."

Ingmar laughs. It is the middle of the week, when we are all at our best. It is a long time since we had a break; our anticipation of the next free day has still not disturbed our working routine. Now, for us, it is only the *film*. Most of all for Ingmar, who walks around and is happy. Contentment itself in his slippers and his sweater.

Lights and camera—everything works—everyone is working calmly and relaxed.

I don't know better days—a finer feeling of teamwork. It is days like this, such linked joys, I long for when I am in Hollywood, surrounded by a hundred people.

Day 25

Today Jenny is going to scream. At one time in her childhood there was a scream of sorrow that never came out. Erland, who plays her doctor friend, tries to take her back to this.

Maybe not only to this single cry, but to all she has encapsulated and carried within her:

The hurt, the frightened, the hateful, the hopeless. Just think, here on earth we are a whole army of women with all our silent screams, a whole army of men with their screams. And we hardly hear each other.

Ingmar writes that perhaps there are no words that reach us, that perhaps there is no reality. That reality exists only as a longing.

I don't know. If so, is not *longing* real? The fact that we *wish* to talk to one another about it, yearn to accept our own and others' insecurity.

Day 26

I love technical challenge. Stop on a chalk mark in the middle of a difficult emotional scene. Know all the time where the camera is and in which angle I should be in relation to it.

Feel inside me a voice directing and at the same time surrender to a situation that has never been mine; although from now on it will be part of my life experience, as if it had happened in reality.

Jenny's fear reminds me of something that once was my life. A distant memory from childhood: the fear of dark. The sounds I listened to in the night. Breath I never dared give sound until I almost choked in my bed when I lay and kept it back.

Sighs which were never uttered.

Much of what I have experienced I use in my profession. The fatigue, the disgust, the fear I have known.

Life experiences become acting experiences, which in turn become life experiences.

I scream with Jenny in front of the camera and feel tremendously relieved afterward.

Think what experience one could bring to one's work after death, not to speak of the experience it would bring to living.

Day 27

Friday. Anticipation of excursions, family, boats and summer homes. I have made weekend plans to go to a cabin with some friends. Linn is bringing a sleeping bag. During the week the friends have gone to get the place ready.

But Ingmar has had visions. He doesn't want me to leave. He has dreamed that the film will be interrupted by a mishap of some kind.

I know that I have to stay behind, otherwise Monday will be impossible: Ingmar's suspicious looks when he sees me. Have I a cold, is anything else wrong with me? Am I tired? Is my concentration on the film gone? His attitude is contagious. I will become nervous, forget my lines, be too eager. Do anything so as not to give him a cause to criticize me—and thereby give him every reason.

If I leave, I know that Ingmar's Sunday evening will be apprehensive. He will be pacing up and down at the window to see when and if I return.

I have to stay home.

While the others are planning their activities, I dramatically sit and suffer in a corner and think of all the food I am going to eat over the weekend, when I have waved goodbye to Linn and the others.

I will set a table by the window and throw down one thick chop after the other in full view of Ingmar. I will raise glass after glass of wine and liqueur to his silhouette behind the curtain. And every mouthful of caramel pudding I swallow will be like a stab through the curtain.

Day 28
Jenny is hysterical. She cannot reach anyone. Sees her daughter in a dream. Runs after her, calls to her. The daughter disappears. Jenny stops, screams, leans her head against a wall. That is where the scene is meant to end, but suddenly Jenny begins to bang her head against the wall. Too late, I discover the sharp edge, but cannot stop. The camera rolls. Besides, in her condition, Jenny would never feel pain. She continues to bang, bang, bang.

While Liv stands nervously by and gets bumps on her head.

Day 29
Jenny has a daughter fourteen years old. Today it is her scene.

The young actress is soft and delicate, with a clear voice. It is easy to recognize Linn in her a few years hence, to discover this with tenderness and wistfulness.

I try to picture to myself how I was when I was that young, but I find that my recollection doesn't go back that far.

Sometimes I feel an anger that I shall never be her again, soft again, have all life's potential within me. And before me.

How strange it is to sit looking at her and know that *I* am close to middle age, to see in her eyes that she doesn't understand that I, too, am fourteen, and wish only for a short time to be *her*.

Years pass by so quickly and already form a cleft of time that cannot be recrossed between me and what I once was.

Two little girls are sitting and talking together—but one of them is not seen by the other.

Day 30

Jenny's grandfather is lying in bed. The end is near. His wife is with him, talking quietly into his ear. They are united in a farewell which Jenny is standing outside watching.

Afterward Gunnar talks about death; he himself has been seriously ill, but now he often jokes and talks about the things that used to frighten him.

"My mother used to say that she pictured death as a handsome man coming to get her. The last of them."

Everyone laughs. Gunnar continues: "You know who has the deepest eyes, the broadest smile and the warmest embrace?" Then his eyes focus on me, and far far in them I see more than he says. "I no longer think of death with panic," he says quietly. "If I become old enough and tired enough, death must feel more natural than birth."

Day 31

One of the last days of this filming. Jenny dreams she is present at her own funeral. They have placed her in a coffin. She has flowers in her hair, her hands are folded over her breast and roses are strewn all over her body.

I have to lie absolutely still so as not to disarrange the decoration.

I feel isolated from the others. As if they are frightened by my coffin, no one talks to me. During the break they all go into the library, and I hear the sound of laughter and conversation.

I ask for paper and a pencil. Carefully lift my arms and make some notes.

"Are you lying there writing your memoirs?" Aino asks dryly as she walks by.

There is an American journalist with us who has followed the progress of this film, mostly from his office because Ingmar doesn't allow outsiders in the studio. Today he is an extra. Even for him, who has seen almost everything in Hollywood, it is unusual to see a prima donna writing in a coffin. He notices me. Most of the time he only pays attention to what Ingmar says and thinks and does.

Happy at having human contact at last, I tell him about the book I am writing. He gives me a friendly smile and says we must talk about it later.

That afternoon I run into him in the corridor. He is on his way to the post office and proudly shows me a letter he has written to an American columnist: "Liv is so sweet and amusing. Today she was lying in her coffin writing. She seems to be planning a book. I'm sure it won't be much, but maybe we can find her a good writer who can shape the material. In any event I should think there is enough stuff for a couple of articles."

I turn white with fury and ask him how he could think of sending such a letter without asking me, without knowing what I am doing.

He becomes confused and hurt and says, "Darling, I only wanted to help. I certainly won't send it."

He crumples the paper and throws it into a wastepaper basket.

When he leaves I retrieve it, smooth it out, and keep it.

Day 32

Everyone shows small signs of fatigue.

The film deals with things we usually do not discuss.

Perhaps it is good to have been through it. Good for those who will see the finished product. That we have no way of knowing yet.

Theo Kalifaties says, "You must think about death three times a day. Then there will be fragrance around your grave."

"Are they going to like our film?" I ask Ingmar.

"Regard it as a surgeon's scalpel. Not everyone will welcome it," he replies.

LINN AND I TALK ABOUT LIFE AND DEATH.

I believe we have an answer together, which lies somewhere in our silence as we sit here.

My hands in yours.

Dear Linn.

There were so many demands from the outside, people who wanted part of that time we should have had together. You have been alone with what we had looked forward to sharing between us.

You have had a hectic and stressed mamma who gives you quick hugs. Listens to you, while she drums her fingers impatiently on the table.

I have been tired and asked you not to be persistent with me, because my nerves were on edge.

And I have seen you at times withdraw from me.

Been afraid to call you back. Afraid because my bad conscience has weighed upon me.

Afraid because the exterior success I have had was achieved at the cost of something the two of us might have had together.

Most afraid I am that it will be too late to reach you on the day I can give you all my time.

You shall know that I love you all the time.

Through the years I have struggled with my profession. Tried to find out who I am and why I am.

Your thin little body is as close to life as I have come.

You who are life itself when I touch you and you become heavy and warm and lean against me. When you pat my cheek and say: "Little Mamma," and understand more than I realize.

When you say that I must not be sad, because you are there.

When you make my life richer, just by being.

Dear Linn . . .

A contact which is without words and without touch.

I stand by the window and see you dig in the soil in pants that are worn at the knees and the bottom.

You have thoughts and adventures I shall never share. I stand and look at you and am closer to you than anything else I know about.

You are a part of me which is completely free.

And I watch you, wishing I had the time to follow you more closely. See how your freedom lives in you.

Do you understand, dear Linn—out there with the children you laugh with and the secret games you play alone, and the fragrances and the colors and all the beauty which is still your world—do you understand that I really have no valid reason not to run out to you and live your life?

It may be the lost kingdom of childhood I am in constant search for.

The text of this book was set on the Linotype in Fairfield, a typeface designed by the distinguished American artist and engraver Rudolph Ruzicka. This type displays the sober and sane qualities of a master craftsman whose talent has long been dedicated to clarity. Rudolph Ruzicka was born in Bohemia in 1883 and came to America in 1894. He has designed and illustrated many books and has created a considerable list of individual prints in a variety of techniques.

Typography and binding design by Camilla Filancia

HB1G